Vocabulary Power Plus for the ACT

Vocabulary, Reading, and Writing Exercises for High Scores

Level Nine

By Daniel A. Reed

Edited by Paul Moliken

Prestwick House

P.O. Box 658 • Clayton, DE 19938
(800) 932-4593 • www.prestwickhouse.com

ISBN   978-1-935467-05-2

Level Nine

Vocabulary
Power Plus
for the
ACT
Vocabulary,
Reading, and Writing
Exercises for High Scores

•Table of Contents•

Vocabulary
Power Plus
for the ACT
Vocabulary,
Reading, and Writing
Exercises for High Scores

·Introduction·

VOCABULARY POWER PLUS FOR THE ACT combines classroom tested vocabulary drills with reading and writing exercises designed to prepare students for the American College Testing assessment; however, *Vocabulary Power Plus for the ACT* is a resource for all students—not just those who are college bound or preparing for the ACT. This series is intended to increase vocabulary, improve grammar, enhance writing, and boost critical reading skills for students at all levels of learning.

Vocabulary lessons combine words-in-context exercises with inferences to ensure that definitions are understood, instead of merely memorized.

Lengthy critical reading exercises and detailed questions emulate the reading passages of the ACT Reading test. Each passage involves a topic in social studies, natural science, prose fiction, or humanities, and is accompanied by multiple levels of questions.

ACT-style grammar passages and questions provide practice in punctuation, usage, structure, and word choice.

The process-oriented writing exercises in *Vocabulary Power Plus for the ACT* develop speed and thrift in essay writing, qualifiable with the objective writing fundamentals in the simulated ACT essay scoring guide.

We hope that you find the *Vocabulary Power Plus for the ACT* series to be an effective tool for teaching new words and an exceptional tool for preparing for the ACT.

Strategies for Completing Activities

Roots, Prefixes, and Suffixes

A knowledge of roots, prefixes, and suffixes can give readers the ability to view unfamiliar words as puzzles that require only a few simple steps to solve. For the person interested in the history of words, this knowledge provides the ability to track word origin and evolution. For those who seek to improve vocabulary, this knowledge creates a sure and lifelong method; however, there are two points to remember:

1. Some words have evolved through usage, so present definitions might differ from what you infer through an examination of the roots and prefixes. The word *abstruse*, for example, contains the prefix *ab* (away) and the root *trudere* (to thrust), and literally means *to thrust away*. Today, *abstruse* is used to describe something that is hard to understand.

2. Certain roots do not apply to all words that use the same form. If you know that the root *vin* means "to conquer," then you would be correct in concluding that the word *invincible* means "incapable of being conquered"; however, if you tried to apply the same root meaning to *vindicate* or *vindictive*, you would be incorrect. When analyzing unfamiliar words, check for other possible roots if your inferred meaning does not fit the context.

Despite these considerations, a knowledge of roots and prefixes is one of the best ways to build a powerful vocabulary.

Critical Reading

Reading questions generally fall into several categories.

1. *Identifying the main idea or the author's purpose.* Generally, the question will ask, "What is this selection about?"

In some passages, the author's purpose will be easy to identify because one or two ideas leap from the text; however, other passages might not be so easily analyzed, especially if they include convoluted sentences. Inverted sentences (subject at the end of the sentence) and elliptical sentences (words missing) will also increase the difficulty of the passages, but all of these obstacles can be overcome if readers take one sentence at a time and recast it in their own words. Consider the following sentence:

These writers either jot down their thoughts bit by bit, in short, ambiguous, and paradoxical sentences, which apparently mean much more than they say—of this kind of writing Schelling's treatises on natural philosophy are a splendid instance; or else they hold forth with a deluge of words and the most intolerable diffusiveness, as though no end of fuss were necessary to make the reader understand the deep meaning of their sentences, whereas it is some quite simple if not actually trivial idea, examples of which may be found in plenty in the popular works of Fichte, and the philosophical manuals of a hundred other miserable dunces.

If we edit out some of the words, the main point of this sentence is obvious.

These writers either jot down their thoughts bit by bit, in short, sentences, which apparently mean much more than they say

or
they hold   a deluge of words
        as though   necessary to make the
reader understand the deep meaning of their sentences

Some sentences need only a few deletions for clarification, but others require major recasting and additions; they must be read carefully and put into the reader's own words.

Some in their discourse desire rather commendation of wit, in being able to hold all arguments, than of judgment, in discerning what is true; as if it were a praise to know what might be said, and not what should be thought.

After studying it, a reader might recast the sentence as follows:

In conversation, some people desire praise for their abilities to maintain the conversation rather than for their abilities to identify what is true or false, as though it were better to sound good than to know what is truth or fiction.

2. Identifying the stated or implied meaning. *What is the author stating or suggesting?*

The literal meaning of a text does not always correspond with the intended meaning. To understand a passage fully, readers must determine which meaning—if there is more than one—is the intended meaning of the passage.

Consider the following sentence:

> If his notice was sought, an expression of courtesy and interest gleamed out upon his features; proving that there was light within him and that it was only the outward medium of the intellectual lamp that obstructed the rays in their passage.

Interpreted literally, this Nathaniel Hawthorne metaphor suggests that a light-generating lamp exists inside of the human body. Since this is impossible, the reader must look to the metaphoric meaning of the passage to properly understand it. In the metaphor, Hawthorne refers to the human mind—consciousness—as a lamp that emits light, and other people cannot always see the lamp because the outside "medium"—the human body—sometimes blocks it.

3. Identifying the tone or mood of the selection. *What feeling does the text evoke?*

To answer these types of questions, readers must look closely at individual words and their connotations; for example, the words *stubborn* and *firm* have almost the same definition, but a writer who describes a character as *stubborn* rather than *firm* is probably suggesting something negative about the character.

Writing

The ACT writing exam allocates only thirty minutes to the composition of a well-organized, fully developed essay. Writing a satisfactory essay in this limited time requires the ability to quickly determine a thesis, organize ideas, and produce adequate examples to support the ideas.

An essay written in thirty minutes might not represent the best process writing—an ACT essay might lack the perfection and depth that weeks of proofreading and editing give to research papers. Process is undoubtedly important, but students must consider the time constraints of the ACT. Completion of the essay is just as important as organization, development, and language use.

The thesis, the organization of ideas, and the support make the framework of a good essay. Before the actual writing begins, a writer must create a mental outline by establishing a thesis, or main idea, and one or more specific supporting ideas (the number of ideas will depend on the length and content of the essay). Supporting ideas should not be overcomplicated; they are simply ideas that justify or explain the thesis. The writer must introduce and explain each supporting idea, and the resultant supporting paragraph should answer the *why?* or *who cares?* questions that the thesis may evoke.

Once the thesis and supporting ideas are identified, writers must determine the order in which the ideas will appear in the essay. A good introduction usually explains the thesis and briefly introduces the supporting ideas. Explanation of the supporting ideas should follow, with each idea in its own paragraph. The final paragraph, the conclusion, usually restates the thesis or summarizes the main ideas of the essay.

Adhering to this mental outline when the writing begins will help the writer organize and develop the essay. Using the Organization and Development scoring guides to evaluate practice essays will help to reinforce the process skills. The Word Choice and Sentence Formation scoring guides will help to strengthen language skills—the vital counterpart to essay organization and development.

Pronunciation Guide

a — track
ā — mate
ä — father
â — care
e — pet
ē — be
i — bit
ī — bite
o — job
ō — wrote
ô — port, horse, **fought**
ōō — proof
ŏŏ — book
u — pun
ū — **you**
û — purr
ə — about, system, supper, circus
îr — steer
ë — Fr. coeur
oi — toy

Word List

Lesson 1
alienate
elated
epigram
fatalistic
lackadaisical
licentious
numismatist
obtrude
paucity
pensive

Lesson 2
amalgamate
antiquated
beleaguer
caricature
dally
demented
felonious
gorge
hone
opiate

Lesson 3
ambidextrous
animate
belated
berserk
chauvinist
delude
edifice
egalitarian
knead
ostentatious

Lesson 4
blight
denizen
elude
entice
fallow
fealty
gambit
gratify
laggard
obsequy

Lesson 5
advocate
bandy
charisma
dastardly
efface
entity
gist
jaded
mesmerize
ogre

Lesson 6
begrudge
bibliophile
declaim
enmity
gaff
glutinous
imbue
mandarin
nepotism
quaff

Lesson 7
cadaverous
daunt
despot
egress
felicity
flux
gird
gothic
hovel
penury

Lesson 8
allude
beget
chafe
desist
educe
effrontery
elite
feign
glean
imbibe

Lesson 9
aghast
bilk
choleric
decadence
demise
emit
eradicate
fabricate
ghastly
granary
homily
impede
lampoon
narcissistic
qualm

Lesson 10
affiliate
bane
berate
blatant
calumny
dawdle
desolate
fallible
fawn
filch
garble
minion
neophyte
pacify
prevaricate

Lesson 11
carp
emissary
facade
flagrant
fracas
futile
gait
genesis
immaculate
kindred
lacerate
nefarious
patrician
query
queue

Lesson 12
anthropomorphic
aplomb
beneficiary
careen
catholic
deluge
eerie
fester
guile
havoc
languish
martial
modicum
pall
rancid

Lesson 13
anachronism
defunct
denigrate
effusive
embroil
envisage
gape
haughty
holocaust
humane
impertinent
lackey
lament
lethal
nemesis

Lesson 14
alacrity
benediction
carnage
catalyst
deify
epitaph
foible
frivolous
harp
impel
impetuous
jargon
judicious
lateral
pallid

Lesson 15
adjunct
chicanery
debonair
deplete
equivocal
farcical
feisty
filial
genealogy
gull
impervious
macabre
mitigate
nadir
penchant

Lesson 16
admonish
affliction
aphorism
cache
daub
delete
impermeable
imperturbable
lax
mendicant
obeisance
oscillate
oust
paean
palpable

Lesson 17
aloof
bias
cavort
desecrate
ensue
fiat
fidelity
fluent
gyrate
hilarity
melee
pariah
pedagogue
personification
rambunctious

Lesson 18
allocate
belabor
conjecture
faux
foray
genocide
gratis
manifesto
materialistic
monolithic
predilection
progeny
quintessential
rudimentary
zaftig

Lesson 19
amenable
conducive
influx
junta
mollify
patina
perjury
pinnacle
placebo
plaintive
rigorous
sedentary
stricture
subversive
tantamount

Lesson 20
acumen
concurrent
erroneous
impasse
irrevocable
malodorous
nanotechnology
negligible
notarize
piquant
precept
pungent
renege
visage
wunderkind

Lesson 21
botch
brinkmanship
confute
dynasty
forte
fortitude
ineffable
kleptomania
meritorious
mezzanine
perennial
purport
recumbent
renown
tribulation

Vocabulary
Power Plus
for the
ACT Vocabulary,
Reading, and Writing
Exercises for High Scores

Lesson One

1. **licentious** (lī sen´ shəs) *adj.* morally unrestrained
   Like St. Augustine, some people want to abandon their *licentious* lifestyles,
   but not immediately.
   syn: immoral; lewd   *ant: chaste; pure*

2. **numismatist** (nōō miz´ mə tist) *n.* a coin collector
   My father is a *numismatist* who has hundreds of coins from ancient Rome.

3. **paucity** (pô´ si tē) *n.* a scarcity, lack
   The *paucity* of jobs in the small town forced Jack to find work elsewhere.
   syn: insufficiency   *ant: abundance*

4. **fatalistic** (fāt əl is´ tik) *adj.* believing that all events in life are
   inevitable and determined by fate
   Fatalistic thinkers believe that there is nothing they can do to change the
   course of their lives.

5. **obtrude** (əb trōōd´) *v.* to force oneself into a situation uninvited
   You were concentrating intently at the work on your desk, so I did not
   wish to *obtrude*.
   syn: impose; intrude   *ant: extricate*

6. **pensive** (pen´ siv) *adj.* dreamily thoughtful
   Jane was in a *pensive* mood after she finished reading the thought-
   provoking novel.
   syn: reflective; meditative   *ant: silly; frivolous*

7. **lackadaisical** (lak ə dā´ zi kəl) *adj.* uninterested; listless
   The *lackadaisical* student sat in the detention hall and stared out the
   window.
   syn: spiritless; apathetic; languid   *ant: enthusiastic; inspired*

8. **alienate** (ā´ lē yə nāt) *v.* to turn away feelings or affections
   Your sarcastic remarks might *alienate* your friends and family.
   syn: estrange; set against   *ant: endear; unite*

9. **elated** (i lā´ tid) *adj.* in high spirits; exultantly proud and joyful
   We were *elated* to learn that our team would move on to finals.
   syn: overjoyed   *ant: depressed*

10. **epigram** (ep´ i gram) *n.* a witty saying expressing a single thought
    or observation
    The author placed relevant *epigrams* at the beginning of each chapter.
    syn: aphorism; bon mot; quip

> ## Exercise I

Words in Context

From the list below, supply the words needed to complete the paragraph. Some words will not be used.

alienate	epigram	fatalistic	licentious
obtrude	lackadaisical	paucity	

1. Byron's _____ notion that he possessed no control over his decisions eventually became his excuse for living a[n] _____ lifestyle. He partied nightly, and his _____ of ambition or goals had _____ him from his relatively successful friends. When they tried to talk to Byron about his future, his only response was a[n] _____ stare.

From the list below, supply the words needed to complete the paragraph. Some words will not be used.

elated	obtrude	alienate	numismatist
pensive	epigram	paucity	

2. Jenny, who lives by Ben Franklin's _____, "Early to bed and early to rise, makes a man healthy, wealthy, and wise," arrived at the flea market at six a.m. It took her two hours to find what she was looking for—a pre-Revolution Era silver dollar. A[n] _____ elderly woman sat behind the stand in the shade of a canvas tarp, reading a leather-bound novel.
   "I'm sorry to _____," said Jenny, "but what are you asking for this old coin?" The old woman looked up from her book, smiled, and said, "Make me an offer." As an experienced _____, Jenny knew the exact value of the coin. She offered half, and Jenny was _____ when the woman accepted her offer.

Exercise II

Sentence Completion

Complete the sentence in a way that shows you understand the meaning of the italicized vocabulary word.

1. You might *alienate* your friends if you...

2. A *numismatist* might spend his or her evenings...

3. If you were not invited to the party, then don't *obtrude* by...

4. One *epigram* that applies to hard work is...

5. The *lackadaisical* player was cut from the team because...

6. Someone who suffers a *paucity* of willpower might find it difficult to...

7. It is *fatalistic* to think that you will...

8. Bill was *elated* to learn that...

9. The *licentious* soldier was court-martialed for...

10. Myra became *pensive* when Cal told her that she...

Exercise III

Roots, Prefixes, and Suffixes

Study the entries and answer the questions that follow.

The prefix *pro* means "before" or "in front."
The roots *fab* and *fess* mean "to speak."
The roots *hab* and *hib* mean "to have" or "to possess."

1. *Using literal translations as guidance, define the following words without using a dictionary.*

    A. inhabit   D. affable
    B. inhibition   E. confab
    C. prohibit   F. fabulist

2. A[n] _____ is a tendency to repeat a particular behavior that you might have, and it is often hard to rid yourself of it. If you have a painting that you want people to see, you might _____ it in an art gallery.

3. At college, a[n] _____ might stand in front of a classroom and speak to students. A short story that often features talking animals and a moral is called a[n] _____.

4. List as many words as you can think of that contain the prefix *pro*.

Exercise IV

Inference

Complete the sentences by inferring information about the italicized word from its context.

1. Wayne always *obtrudes* upon our conversations, so if we want to discuss something privately, we should…

2. Two prisoners escaped because the *lackadaisical* guard was…

3. Japan is an industrial power, but its *paucity* of natural resources forces the nation to…

Exercise V

Writing

Here is a writing prompt similar to the one you will find on the essay writing portion of the ACT.

> Increases in childhood food allergies have resulted in some schools banning the possession of traditional lunch food, most popularly peanut butter, citing the possible deadly consequences if it were to come into contact with an allergic student and the proper treatment were not provided quickly enough. Because peanut butter is such a long-lived and popular product, the bans are always controversial, generating complaints from angry parents over the changing of school policies for the accommodation of a very small percentage of students. Those who disagree with the bans suggest that the affected students change their own routines to protect themselves from allergens rather than force changes upon the majority.
>
> Are peanut bans, or equivalent bans, fair practice for schools, or should allergies or similar maladies be handled at the individual level, as the critics suggest? Should the majority be inconvenienced to protect the few, or should the few be assured that they will be provided a safe environment no matter what the cost to others?
>
> Take a side in the argument and write a letter to your school board in favor of or against food bans. Support your argument with at least three subtopics. Your support can be based on your own experience, reading, observations, or reasoning.

Thesis: Write a *one-sentence* response to the above assignment. Make certain this single sentence offers a clear statement of your position.

Example: While the practice seems unfair to the majority, bans are necessary when they involve life-and-death situations.

_____

_____

Organizational Plan: List at least three subtopics you will use to support your main idea. This list is your outline.

1. _____

2. _____

3. _____

Draft: Following your outline, write a good first draft of your essay. Remember to support all your points with examples, facts, references to reading, etc.

Review and Revise: Exchange essays with a classmate. Using the scoring guide for Organization on page 216, score your partner's essay (while he or she scores yours). Focus on the organizational plan and use of language conventions. If necessary, rewrite your essay to improve the organizational plan and/or your use of language.

Exercise VI

English Practice

Identifying Sentence Errors

*Identify the errors in the following sentences. Choose the answer that fixes the error.
If the sentence contains no error, select NO CHANGE.*

1. <u>Her sister and her are</u> now employed at Beef Barn as cooks.
   A. NO CHANGE
   B. Her sister and her is
   C. She and her sister are
   D. She and her sister is

2. <u>While dad slept the toddlers</u> wrote on the walls with crayons.
   F. NO CHANGE
   G. While dad slept, the toddlers
   H. While dad slept the toddlers
   J. While dad slept, the toddlers,

3. An important function of helicopters <u>are</u> search and rescue capability.
   A. NO CHANGE
   B. were
   C. seem to be
   D. is

4. The mechanic told Bill and <u>I that the car</u> was not finished.
   F. NO CHANGE
   G. I, that the car
   H. me that the car
   J. I that the car,

5. <u>Greg only threw the shot put</u> twenty feet.
   A. NO CHANGE
   B. Greg threw the shot put only
   C. Only Greg threw the shot put
   D. Greg threw only the shot put

Improving Sentences

The underlined portion of each sentence below contains some flaw. Select the answer that best corrects the flaw.

6. Jillian could have cared less about the score of the hockey game.
    F. could haven't cared less
    G. couldn't have cared less
    H. could have cared as much
    J. could not care

7. Going to school is preferable than going to work.
    A. preferable
    B. preferably
    C. preferable to
    D. more preferable

8. Wild and vicious, the veterinarian examined the wounded panther.
    F. The wild and vicious wounded panther was examined by the veterinarian.
    G. The veterinarian examined the wounded, wild, and vicious panther.
    H. The wild and vicious veterinarian examined the wounded panther.
    J. Wild and vicious, the examined panther wounded the veterinarian.

9. Journalists are stimulated by his or her deadline.
    A. A journalist are
    B. Journalism is
    C. Journalists is
    D. A journalist is

10. When someone has been drinking, they are more likely to speed.
    F. a person has
    G. a driver has
    H. someone have
    J. drivers have

Vocabulary
Power Plus
for the **ACT**
Vocabulary,
Reading, and Writing
Exercises for High Scores

Lesson Two

1. **amalgamate** (ə malʹ gə māt) *v.* to combine
The great leader *amalgamated* many small tribes into his own to make a single, powerful nation.
syn: unite; blend; merge; consolidate   *ant: splinter; disunite*

2. **demented** (di menʹ tid) *adj.* mentally ill; insane
Mary's *demented* cat attacks anything that makes a noise, including the television.
syn: deranged; insane   *ant: sane*

3. **hone** (hōn) *v.* to sharpen
The butcher used a whetstone to *hone* his knives until they were razor sharp.
                                    ant: dull

4. **beleaguer** (bi lēʹ gər) *v.* to besiege by encircling (as with an army); to harass
The mosquitoes will *beleaguer* you if you venture near the swamp.
syn: surround; annoy   *ant: evade*

5. **gorge** (gôrj) *v.* to eat or swallow greedily
The beagle *gorged* itself after it chewed through the bag containing the dog food.

6. **antiquated** (anʹ ti kwā tid) *adj.* no longer used or useful; very old
The *antiquated* washboard hung on the wall, useful only as a decoration.
syn: obsolete; out-of-date; archaic   *ant: modern*

7. **opiate** (ōʹ pē it) *n.* a narcotic used to cause sleep or bring relief from pain
The veterinarian used an *opiate* to sedate the wounded animal.
                                ant: stimulant

8. **caricature** (karʹ i kə chûr) *n.* an exaggerated portrayal of one's features
The *caricature* of the mayor in the political cartoon exaggerated the size of his ears and nose.
syn: mockery; cartoon

9. **dally** (dal´ ē) *v.* to waste time; to dawdle
If you *dally* too long in making a decision, someone else will buy the car you want.
syn: dawdle; loiter   ant: hasten; hurry

10. **felonious** (fə lō´ nē əs) *adj.* pertaining to or constituting a major crime
The inmate expected to be released from prison early, despite the many *felonious* activities on his record.
syn: criminal

Exercise I

Words in Context

From the list below, supply the words needed to complete the paragraph. Some words will not be used.

antiquated	gorge	caricature	felonious
opiate	dally	beleaguer	

1. Alex crouched behind a palm tree and shook her head; she had escaped from her cell, but she was still woozy from the _____ that her captors used to drug her. She didn't _____, because the guards would be searching for her in a matter of minutes. Knowing that it might be days before she would eat again, Alex _____ herself on a bag lunch that one of the guards had left unattended near her cell. Seconds later, she began looking for the _____ truck that the guards had used to transport her to the compound. She knew that the outmoded vehicle wouldn't set any speed records, but it was her only option for getting back to civilization. The odds were against Alex, but she had to make it out of the jungle before she could expose the drug kingpin's _____ operation to the public.

From the list below, supply the words needed to complete the paragraph. Some words will not be used.

dally	caricature	beleaguer	hone
amalgamate	felonious	demented	

2. Doctor Rearick, a famous chemist, mused at the _____ of himself in the editorial cartoon. The artist had depicted the aging chemist as a[n] _____ scientist, like Victor Frankenstein or Doctor Moreau, at a lab table trying to _____ two mysterious liquids by pouring them both into a steaming test tube. Reporters _____ him with phone calls for days after he announced the discovery of a remarkable new alloy, and Rearick knew that he would need to _____ his public speaking skills before he explained the full significance of the discovery in front of the television news cameras.

Exercise II

Sentence Completion

Complete the sentence in a way that shows you understand the meaning of the italicized vocabulary word.

1. The doctor administered an *opiate* to the patient to...

2. If you *dally* in finishing your report, you might...

3. People think that she's *demented* just because she...

4. The political cartoonist's *caricature* depicted the president as...

5. The seagulls *beleaguered* the people on the beach until...

6. You should first *hone* your skills if you plan to...

7. The teacher told us not to *amalgamate* those chemicals because...

8. Bert *gorged* himself at the buffet because he...

9. Andy's *felonious* behavior finally caught up to him when...

10. Paul replaced his *antiquated* computer because it...

Exercise III

Roots, Prefixes, and Suffixes

Study the entries and answer the questions that follow.

The prefix *sub* means "under" or "below."
The suffix *ize* means "to make."
The root *urb* means "city."

1. *Using literal translations as guidance, define the following words without using a dictionary.*

   A. suburb   D. standardize
   B. urbanize   E. subhuman
   C. substandard   F. humanize

2. A[n] _____ is a vessel that travels underwater, and a *subway* train travels _____ the ground.

3. List as many words as you can think of that contain the prefix *sub* or the suffix *ize*.

Exercise IV

Inference

Complete the sentences by inferring information about the italicized word from its context.

1. If Kevin needs a large bowl to *amalgamate* the ingredients, he is probably going to...

2. If an angry mob *beleaguered* the driver of the car, then the driver was probably...

3. Nolan went to the library to *hone* his understanding of chemistry by...

Exercise V

Critical Reading

Below is a reading passage followed by several multiple-choice questions similar to the ones you will encounter on the ACT. Carefully read the passage and choose the best answer for each of the questions.

The author of the following passage explains recent astronomical discoveries and their significance to humanity.

1   Humans have fantasized about the significance of planets ever since the ancients first identified the "wandering stars." Planets are fundamental to mythology and astrology, and as we indulge our imaginations on the future of humanity, planets are essential to our vision of interstellar endeavors, both in fiction and in fact. Recent discoveries have revealed plenty of new material for our imaginations. Our civilization may lack the technology to set foot on the unexplored planets of our own solar system, but that won't prevent us from compiling a list of new planets to explore when we finally do have the technology.

2   In 1991, Alexander Wolszczan, an astronomy professor from Penn State University, used a radio telescope to time signals that revealed three planets orbiting a very distant pulsar. Located more than 1000 light years from Earth in the constellation Virgo, two of the planets resemble Earth in density, while the third is moon-sized. The probability of life on these planets is low; due to their proximity to the pulsar, the planets endure a constant bombardment of radiation that would render them inhospitable. The planets are probably barren, lifeless worlds, but such speculation is only secondary to the paramount discovery: planets exist elsewhere in the galaxy. Their simple existence is enough to confirm that our own solar system is only one of possible billions elsewhere in the galaxy—and we have the means to detect them.

3   The next major extrasolar planet discovery occurred in 1995, when Michel Mayor and Didier Queloz used spectrographic data to discover a large planet orbiting 51 Pegasi, a star that resembles our own sun. The planet is likely a gas giant similar to our own Jupiter, but its correlation with a sun-like star inspires high hopes that a solar system like our own will eventually be found.

4   Since 1995, astronomers have added more than 700 new planets to their list of discoveries, some of which exist in multiple-planet systems. Most of the discovered planets are Jovian, as that of the 51 Pegasi system, but that, astronomers stress, is due to our limited detection methods.

5   Extrasolar planets are invisible to optical telescopes. Researchers instead rely upon the behavior of parent stars to signal the presence of planets. As any planet orbits a star, the two bodies pull toward each other due to gravity. For an observer who has a side view of the celestial process, the parent star will appear to "wobble." All stars with planets exhibit this behavior, but large planets that orbit close to their parent stars cause enough wobble that we can detect it from hundreds of light years away. By identifying and measuring the wobble of the parent stars, astronomers confirm the presence of planets and calculate planetary mass.

6   Discoveries become increasingly noteworthy as astronomers refine extrasolar detection techniques. At the time in which the first pulsar planets were discovered, researchers found mainly gas giants in close proximity to the parent stars. Researchers are now discovering planetary systems that contain increasingly smaller planets with longer orbits. The significance? As we discover planetary systems with smaller planets further from their parent stars, we approach the day in which we find the smallest of planets: terrestrial planets, like Earth. Where terrestrial planets exist, conditions for known forms of life could exist. The discovery of extraterrestrial life could reroute the collective attention, philosophies, and endeavors of our civilization.

7   Even if we are unable to find any terrestrial planets, astronomers theorize that our next major extrasolar discovery might be that of planetary satellites. If the Jovian planets that have been discovered are anything like Jupiter and Saturn, then there is a probability that they will have satellites—Jupiter has thirty-nine known satellites, and Saturn has at least eighteen. Some of the satellites in our solar system, such as Saturn's Titan and Jupiter's Io, have atmospheres. The satellite atmospheres in our solar system might be inhospitable to life, but what about the satellites of the newly discovered giants?

8   Is it possible that a satellite of one of the newly discovered planets, 300 light years away, could have atmospheric conditions like those of our nurturing Earth? Time and technology will tell, but at least we now know, thanks to early extrasolar explorers, where to direct our attention in the human quest for answers.

1. The primary purpose of this passage is to
    A. offer theories on the formation of planets.
    B. explain how new planets are detected.
    C. discuss the impact of new discoveries.
    D. inform readers about the discovery of new planets.

2. The overall tone of this passage is
    F. descriptive.
    G. humorous.
    H. optimistic.
    J. simplistic.

3. Which of the following would be the best substitute for *proximity* in paragraph 2?
    A. size
    B. remoteness
    C. gravitational pull
    D. nearness

4. According to paragraph 2, why are the pulsar planets probably devoid of life?
    F. The pulsar bombards the planets with radiation.
    G. The pulsar creates extreme temperatures on the planets.
    H. The planets lack atmospheres.
    J. The planets rotate too quickly.

5. As used in paragraph 4, the word *Jovian* most nearly means
    A. joyous.
    B. mythological.
    C. resembling Jupiter.
    D. nonexistent.

6. According to paragraph 5, astronomers discover mostly large planets because
    F. Earth has no telescopes beyond the atmosphere.
    G. small planets do not cause enough wobble to detect from Earth.
    H. small planets burn up while orbiting the parent stars.
    J. the atmospheres of small planets obscure the images.

7. In paragraph 7, the author lists the known numbers of satellites for Jupiter and Saturn because
    A. it increases the likelihood that the new planets will have satellites.
    B. it impresses the audience with statistics.
    C. it describes how Jupiter and Saturn are unlike the discovered planets.
    D. it provides an example that supports the new planets having satellites.

8. Which of the following best describes this passage?
    F. specific and explanatory
    G. conjectural and cynical
    H. abridged and speculative
    J. thorough and comprehensive

9. What would make the best title for this passage?
    A. Techniques of Planetary Detection
    B. The Search for Life
    C. The Space Frontier: Specks on the Horizon
    D. Astronomers Find Planets

10. This passage would most likely be found in a/an
    F. encyclopedia.
    G. fiction novel.
    H. history book.
    J. exploration magazine.

Vocabulary Power Plus
for the **ACT**
Vocabulary, Reading, and Writing Exercises for High Scores

Lesson Three

1. **edifice** (ed´ ə fis) *n.* a large, elaborate structure; an imposing building
    The palace was not just a home; it was an *edifice* that created envy among foreign rulers.
    syn: fortress   *ant: hovel*

2. **ambidextrous** (am bi dek´ strəs) *adj.* equally skillful with either hand
    The *ambidextrous* woman could write both left- and right-handed.

3. **belated** (bi lā´ tid) *adj.* delayed
    Joan sent a *belated* birthday card to her sister.
    syn: tardy; late ant: timely

4. **animate** (an´ ə māt) *v.* to give life or motion to
    A trip to the ice cream parlor helped to *animate* the sullen child.
    syn: enliven; encourage; excite   *ant: quell*

5. **knead** (nēd) *v.* to work dough or clay into a uniform mixture
    It is easier to *knead* dough with an electric mixer than by hand.
    syn: squeeze; rub; press

6. **chauvinist** (shō´ və nist) *n.* one having a fanatical devotion to a country, gender, or religion, with contempt for other countries, the opposite sex, or other beliefs
    He did not dislike women, but he was a *chauvinist* when it came to hiring women for management positions.

7. **egalitarian** (i gal i ter´ ē ən) *adj.* promoting equal rights for all people
    The equal rights amendment for women was founded on *egalitarian* principles.
    ant: elitist

8. **berserk** (bər sûrk´) *adj.* in a state of violent or destructive rage
    My father almost went *berserk* when I told him I had dented his new car.
    syn: frenzied   *ant: placid; complacent*

9. **ostentatious** (os ten tā´ shəs) *adj.* marked by a conspicuous, showy, or pretentious display
The *ostentatious* charity ball cost the guests $2,000 per plate.
syn: grandiose   *ant: unobtrusive; bland*

10. **delude** (di lood´) *v.* to mislead; to fool
The fast-talking salesman could not *delude* us into buying the dilapidated truck.
syn: deceive   *ant: enlighten*

Exercise I

Words in Context

From the list below, supply the words needed to complete the paragraph. Some words will not be used.

delude   edifice   berserk   ostentatious   animate

1. The old Lane estate was a[n] _____ that towered over the other homes in the neighborhood. It had a[n] _____ courtyard more suitable for a palace, and rows of shimmering Aspen trees seemed to _____ the grounds when they fluttered with even the mildest breeze. The elaborate exterior of the mansion might _____ someone into thinking that the house must be beautiful inside, but actually, the roof leaks, the paint is peeling, and the floors creak.

From the list below, supply the words needed to complete the paragraph. Some words will not be used.

chauvinist   ostentatious   belated   egalitarian

2. The corporation claimed to endorse _____ company policies, but some of the managers were _____ who refused to promote anyone not native to Scandinavia. One of the foreign employees eventually filed suit against the company, and in two years was awarded the _____ promotion he had long deserved.

From the list below, supply the words needed to complete the paragraph. Some words will not be used.

ambidextrous   **berserk**   **knead**   **edifice**

3.   Laurie _____ the modeling clay until it was soft enough to work with. Since her work required deep concentration, she nearly went _____ when her assistant interrupted for the third time to obtain Laurie's signature. Even though Laurie was _____, she could not sign her name and focus on her art simultaneously.

Exercise II

Sentence Completion

Complete the sentence in a way that shows you understand the meaning of the italicized vocabulary word.

1.   Janet bought a *belated* graduation gift for Mike because she…

2.   The *ambidextrous* pitcher could throw…

3.   In an *egalitarian* nation, everyone has the…

4.   One *edifice* that most people have seen in pictures is…

5.   The soccer player *kneaded* her calf muscle because…

6.   Though he was quite wealthy, the miser's home lacked *ostentatious* artwork or furniture because he…

7.   The sound of food pouring into a metal dish *animated*…

8.   Uncle Phil was admittedly a male *chauvinist* who believed that…

9.   Don't let the resort's brochure *delude* you; we went there last year, and the pictures in the guide are…

10. Rabies caused the dog to act *berserk*, so…

Exercise III

Roots, Prefixes, and Suffixes

Study the entries and answer the questions that follow.

The roots *mater* and *matr* mean "mother."
The root *micro* means "small."
The root *meter* means "measure."
The root *aut* means "self."

1. *Using literal translations as guidance, define the following words without using a dictionary.*

    A. alma mater
    B. matron
    C. matrimony
    D. microprocessor
    E. micrometer
    F. automatic

2. Mothers are known to have certain _____ instincts, especially with regard to caring for their children. In a *matriarchal* society, family lineage is traced through the _____'s side of the family instead of the father's side.

3. If *cosmos* means "world," then a *microcosm* must be _____.
    Microbes are so _____ that you need a[n] _____ to see them.

4. List as many words as you can think of that contain the roots *meter* or *auto*.

Exercise IV

Inference

Complete the sentences by inferring information about the italicized word from its context.

1. If the mad doctor wants to try to *animate* the lifeless monster, then he or she wants to...

2. An *ambidextrous* golfer would not need to worry about having left- or right-handed clubs because...

3. If Karen was angry that Mark did not follow through with his *egalitarian* plan, then Mark must have...

Exercise V

Writing

Here is a writing prompt similar to the one you will find on the essay writing portion of the ACT.

During World War II, many fences and store windows throughout the United States were decorated with posters that contained phrases such as "Loose lips sink ships." At the time, the largest military operation in the history of the planet was underway, and the United States was fighting on fronts in two hemispheres. In the meantime, the Manhattan Project—the secret plan to produce an atomic bomb—depended on thousands of people saying nothing in order to prevent the enemy from gaining an advantage or sabotaging the war effort.

By definition, information classified top secret, if released to the public, will cause grave danger to national security. Imagine, for example, a terrorist group learning the top secret launch codes to a nuclear weapon. Not all secrets involve weapons, of course; sometimes the classified data include intelligence collected about international trade, or weaknesses of allied nations. Lesser secrets are expected to be less damaging than top secret, but they are damaging nonetheless. Compromised secrets can shatter alliances, generate hostility, and weaken the nation's trade and commerce.

The spread of Internet "whistleblower" sites, in which anonymous government employees post classified information for the world to see has sparked debate between two governmental ideaologies: those who believe that secrets merely enable tyranny and keep the population intentionally ignorant.

Imagine that you have been appointed Director of National Intelligence of the United States, and that you have influence over the way in which classified information is managed. Take a side in the debate over classified information and address your opposition in a speech, explaining why you do or do not believe that secrets are important to the nation. Support your argument with at least three subtopics derived from your own experience, reading, observations, or reasoning.

Thesis: Write a *one-sentence* response to the above assignment. Make certain this single sentence offers a clear statement of your position.

Example: Secrets are paramount to the country because as a nation, we can trust only ourselves to look after our own interests.

_____

_____

Organizational Plan: List at least three subtopics you will use to support your main idea. This list is your outline.

1. _____

2. _____

3. _____

Draft: Following your outline, write a good first draft of your essay. Remember to support all your points with examples, facts, references to reading, etc.

Review and Revise: Exchange essays with a classmate. Using the scoring guide for Development of Ideas on page 217, score your partner's essay (while he or she scores yours). Focus on the development of ideas and use of language conventions. If necessary, rewrite your essay to incorporate more (or more relevant) support and/or to improve your use of language.

Exercise VI

English Practice

Improving Paragraphs
Read the following passage and then choose the best revision for the underlined portions of the paragraph. The questions will require you to make decisions regarding the revision of the reading selection. Some revisions are not of actual mistakes, but will improve the clarity of the writing.

[1]

We have tried in the <u>proceeding</u>[1] chapters to understand a few of the laws of health and to apply them intelligently to our daily living. It will help us to clinch what we have already mastered, if <u>we supplement our work with a knowledge of simple methods now</u>[2] of procedure in case of the more common and <u>not as</u>[3] serious accidents and emergencies.

1. A. NO CHANGE
   B. progressing
   C. succeeding
   D. preceding

2. F. NO CHANGE
   G. we now supplement our work with a knowledge of simple methods
   H. we supplement our work with a knowledge now of simple methods
   J. we supplement now our work with a knowledge of simple methods

3. A. NO CHANGE
   B. less
   C. lesser
   D. fewer

[2]

Emergencies and accidents are a frequent occurrence. A playmate may cut his leg or foot with a scythe or knife, or fall and <u>have broken</u>[4] his arm. A child may accidentally swallow some laudanum, set his own clothing on fire, or push a bean into his nose or <u>ear, a teamster</u>[5] may be brought in with his ears frostbitten. A small boy may fall into the river and be brought out apparently drowned. A member of our own family <u>may be</u>[6] taken suddenly sick with some contagious disease or may be suffocated with coal gas.

4. F. NO CHANGE
   G. break
   H. broke
   J. breaking

6. F. NO CHANGE
   G. might be
   H. will be
   J. might

5. A. NO CHANGE
   B. ear a teamster
   C. ear—a teamster
   D. ear. A teamster

[3]

All these and many other things of a like nature call for a cool head, a steady hand, <u>and, some practical knowledge,</u>[7] of what is to be done until medical or surgical help <u>was obtained</u>.[8] A fairly good working knowledge of such matters may be easily mastered.

7. A. NO CHANGE
   B. and, some practical knowledge
   C. and some practical knowledge
   D. and; some practical knowledge

8. F. NO CHANGE
   G. is been obtained
   H. gets obtained
   J. is obtained

[4]

A boy or girl who has acquired this knowledge and <u>whom are able</u>[9] to maintain a certain amount of self-control will find many opportunities in later years <u>for to lend</u>[10] a hand in the midst of accidents or sudden sickness.

9. A. NO CHANGE
   B. who are able
   C. able
   D. who is able

10. F. NO CHANGE
    G. to lend
    H. of to lend
    J. to the lending

[5]

(1) All that is expected of us is to tide over matters until the doctor comes. (2) Retain, as far as possible, presence of mind, or, <u>another words</u>,[11] keep cool. (3) Act <u>prompt and quiet</u>,[12] but not with haste. (4) First aid kits have been manufactured since 1890, at the latest.

11.A. NO CHANGE
 B. an other words
 C. in another words
 D. in other words

12.F. NO CHANGE
 G. promptly and quiet
 H. promptly and quietly
 J. prompt and quietly

13.Which sentence should be deleted from paragraph 5 because it deviates from the flow of information?
 A. sentence 1
 B. sentence 2
 C. sentence 3
 D. sentence 4

[6]

Make the sufferer comfortable by <u>providing</u>[14] an abundance of fresh air and placing him in a restful position. Loosen all tight articles of clothing. Such as belts, bindings, corsets, and collars. Be sure to send for a doctor at once if the emergency calls for any such skilled service.

14.F. NO CHANGE
 G. giving the sufferer
 H. them
 J. providing them with

15.In the final paragraph, sentence 3 requires revision because
 A. it contains an unnecessary comma in the series.
 B. it is a fragment, not a sentence.
 C. it contains a pronoun that does not agree with its object.
 D. the clothes listed are all very outdated.

Vocabulary
Power Plus
for the
ACT
Vocabulary,
Reading, and Writing
Exercises for High Scores

Lesson Four

1. **elude** (i lōōd´) *v.* to escape notice; to get away from
The prisoner tried to *elude* the guards by hiding in the laundry truck.
syn: avoid; evade; lose   *ant: attract*

2. **fallow** (fal´ ō) *adj.* inactive; unproductive
A *fallow* mind needs to be stimulated with challenging ideas and projects.
syn: idle; barren   *ant: fertile; productive*

3. **blight** (blīt) *n.* anything that destroys, prevents growth, or causes
devaluation
The junkyard was a *blight* on the otherwise appealing neighborhood.
syn: affliction; disease   *ant: enhancement*

4. **obsequy** (ob´ sə kwē) *n.* a funeral rite or ceremony
The explorers held brief *obsequies* for their fallen leader before burying him
on the side of the mountain.

5. **denizen** (den´ i zən) *n.* an occupant; inhabitant
Prairie dogs are *denizens* of the Great Plains, so it is unlikely that you would
see one in Maine.
syn: resident   *ant: emigrant; alien*

6. **fealty** (fē´ əl tē) *n.* obligated loyalty or faithfulness
Peasants who did not show any *fealty* to the duke often disappeared.
syn: devotion; fidelity; allegiance   *ant: disloyalty; treachery*

7. **entice** (en tīs´) *v.* to attract by offering reward or pleasure
The styling and color of the gown *enticed* me, but I could not afford such
an extravagant purchase.
syn: tempt; lure *ant: discourage*

8. **gratify** (grat´ ə fī) *v.* to please
To *gratify* the pouting child, his mother handed him a lollipop.
syn: satisfy; indulge   *ant: displease; disappoint*

9. **laggard** (lag´ ərd) *n.* a slow person, especially one who falls behind
Wear good shoes on the hike, or you'll be a *laggard* and delay the entire
group.
syn: straggler; dawdler   *ant: leader*

10. **gambit** (gam´ bit) *n.* maneuver or action used to gain an advantage
    The general's *gambit* sacrificed many soldiers, but ultimately won the battle.
    syn: strategy; ploy; maneuver   *ant: blunder*

Exercise I

Words in Context

From the list below, supply the words needed to complete the paragraph. Some words will not be used.

fealty	entice	elude	fallow
blight	denizen	gambit	

1. Overuse of the soil and an extended drought contributed to the _____ known in history as the Dust Bowl. In the Midwest, _____ fields lay barren for a decade, forcing many _____ of the community to give up their farms and seek employment in the cities, where industry _____ them with promises of steady, but ultimately minuscule, paychecks. In the years that followed the Dust Bowl, farmers stopped over-plowing fields because they knew that no one could _____ nature's wrath.

From the list below, supply the words needed to complete the paragraph. Some words will not be used.

laggard	entice	gambit	obsequy
denizen	fealty	gratify	

2. The king knew that his plan for a surprise attack would be a[n] _____ that would test the _____ of his soldiers, but it was the only chance he had of thwarting the invading fleet. Speed would be the key to success; one _____ in the ranks could jeopardize the entire operation if the soldier were not in place at the right time. As an incentive to fight well, the king promised to _____ each soldier with twenty acres of land after the battle. The promise was unprecedented, but on the other hand, if the army should fail, then the soldiers would be lucky to have proper _____ because the invaders did not plan to take prisoners.

Exercise II

Sentence Completion

Complete the sentence in a way that shows you understand the meaning of the italicized vocabulary word.

1. The manager *gratified* the complaining customer by...

2. The oil spill was a *blight* that caused...

3. The villagers had limited *fealty* for the new king because he...

4. Tim tried to *elude* the mosquitoes by...

5. Mikhail's *gambit* during the chess game cost him...

6. Many *denizens* of the beach community like to...

7. The *laggard* didn't get tickets to the concert because he...

8. The brochure *enticed* Annette to visit the island because...

9. The *fallow* economy forced many investors to...

10. Instead of a typical *obsequy*, the dying man requested...

Exercise III

Roots, Prefixes, and Suffixes

Study the entries and answer the questions that follow.

The root *chroma* means "color."
The prefix *mono* means "one."
The prefix *poly* means "many."
The root *morph* means "form" or "shape."

1. *Using literal translations as guidance, define the following words without using a dictionary.*

   A. polychromatic   D. polymorphic
   B. monochromatic   E. monorail
   C. polygon   F. monosyllabic

2. Someone who speaks in a single pitch, whose voice does not raise or lower, is said to speak in a[n] _____. Doing _____ thing might become *monotonous* after a few hours.

3. List as many words as you can think of that contain the prefix *poly* or the root *morph*.

Exercise IV

Inference

Complete the sentences by inferring information about the italicized word from its context.

1. The team would have won the relay race if it had not been for the *laggard* who…

2. The coach's *gambit* left his players vulnerable, but the bold move…

3. If Lonnie tried to *elude* his friends in the mall, then he probably…

Exercise V

Critical Reading

Below is a passage followed by several multiple-choice questions similar to the ones you will encounter on the ACT. Carefully read the passage and choose the best answer to each of the questions.

The following passage is an excerpt of a speech by Hannibal, the renowned Carthaginian general, delivered shortly after the invading Carthaginian army astonished the Romans by crossing the Alps at the start of the Second Punic War.

Hannibal's Speech to his Soldiers (218 B.C.)

If, soldiers, you shall by and by, in judging of your own fortune, preserve the same feelings which you experienced a little before in the example of the fate of the others we have already conquered; for neither was that merely a spectacle, but, as it were, a certain representation of your condition. And I know not whether fortune
5 has not thrown around you still stronger chains and more urgent necessities than around your captives. On the right and left two seas enclose you, without your possessing even a single ship for escape. The river Po around you, the Po larger and more impetuous than the Rhone; the Alps behind, scarcely passed by you when fresh and vigorous, hem you in.

10 Here, soldiers, where you have first met the enemy, you must conquer or die; and the same fortune which has imposed the necessity of fighting holds out to you, if victorious, rewards than which men are not wont to desire greater, even from the immortal gods. If we were only about to recover by our valor Sicily and Sardinia, wrested from our fathers, the recompense would be sufficiently ample; but
15 whatever, acquired and amassed by so many triumphs, the Romans possess, all with its masters themselves, will become yours. To gain this rich reward, hasten, then, and seize your arms, with the favor of the gods.

For, setting aside only the splendor of the Roman name, what remains in which they can be compared to you? To pass over in silence your service for twenty years,
20 distinguished by such valor and success, you have made your way to this place from the pillars of Hercules, from the ocean and the remotest limits of the world, advancing victorious through so many of the fiercest nations of Gaul and Spain; you will fight with a raw army, which this very summer was beaten, conquered, and surrounded by the Gauls, as yet unknown to its general, and ignorant of him. Shall
25 I compare myself—almost born, and certainly bred, in the tent of my father, that most illustrious commander, myself the subjugator of Spain and Gaul, the conqueror too not only of the Alpine nations, but, what is much more, of the Alps themselves—with this six-months' general, the deserter of his army?—to whom, if any one, having taken away their standards, should today show the Carthaginians
30 and Romans, I am sure that he would not know of which army he was consul.

I do not regard it, soldiers, as of small account that there is not a man among you before whose eyes I have not often achieved some military exploit; and to whom, in like manner, I, the spectator and witness of his valor, could not recount his own gallant deeds, particularized by time and place. With soldiers who have a
35 thousand times received my praises and gifts, I, who was the pupil of you all before I became your commander, will march out in battle-array against those who are unknown to and ignorant of each other.

That most cruel and haughty nation considers everything its own, and at its own disposal; it thinks it right that it should regulate with whom we are to have war, with
40 whom peace; it circumscribes and shuts us up by the boundaries of mountains and rivers which we must not pass, and then does not adhere to those boundaries which it appointed. Pass not the Iberus; have nothing to do with the Saguntines. Saguntum is on the Iberus; you must not move a step in any direction. Is it a small thing that you take away my most ancient provinces—Sicily and Sardinia? Will you take Spain
45 also? And should I withdraw thence, you will cross over into Africa.

Will cross, did I say? They have sent the two consuls of this year, one to Africa, the other to Spain: there is nothing left to us in any quarter, except what we can assert to ourselves by arms. Those may be cowards and dastards who have something to look back upon; whom, flying through safe and unmolested roads, their own lands
50 and their own country will receive: there is a necessity for you to be brave, and, since all between victory and death is broken off from you by inevitable despair, either to conquer, or if fortune should waver, to meet death rather in battle than in flight. If this be well fixed and determined in the minds of you all, I will repeat, you have already conquered; no stronger incentive to victory has been given to man by the
55 immortal gods.

1. As used in line 1, *fortune* most nearly means
    A. wealth.
    B. luck.
    C. situation.
    D. victory.

2. Which choice best describes the intent of lines 5–9 in paragraph 1?
    F. to remind the soldiers of their own personal strength
    G. to express the difficulty of crossing the Po River
    H. to warn the soldiers about the Roman Navy
    J. to emphasize that the soldiers cannot turn back

3. What can be inferred from Hannibal's description of the mountains in paragraph 1 as it pertains to the status of the Carthaginian forces?
   A. The soldiers are questing for treasure.
   B. Winter snows have blocked the mountain pass.
   C. The mountains are beyond the sea.
   D. The troops are too exhausted to cross again.

4. As used in line 14, *recompense* most nearly means
   F. restitution.
   G. sacrifice.
   H. expenditure.
   J. revenge.

5. Choose the best explanation, based on the passage, of Hannibal's reference to the fathers of Carthage.
   A. Carthage received money for surrendering Italy.
   B. Hannibal's father was taken prisoner by the Romans.
   C. The Romans took Carthaginian colonies in Sicily before Hannibal's time.
   D. Carthage had previously invaded Italy and paid a large tribute for Sicily.

6. According to Hannibal, the Roman forces
   F. are cowardly and poor, having squandered their wealth.
   G. are formidable and historically victorious.
   H. are incapable of invading territories of Carthage.
   J. are inexperienced and suffering from poor leadership.

7. If Carthage is successful, according to Hannibal, then the *masters* in line 16 will become
   A. the people who control the Roman treasure.
   B. those who defeat the Romans.
   C. favors from the gods.
   D. slaves to the Carthaginians.

8. From his tone in the passage, Hannibal can best be described as
   F. a self-centered tyrant.
   G. a fatherly leader.
   H. blinded by outrage.
   J. cavalier and hasty.

9. Which is *not* one of the reasons Hannibal offers as justification for invading Italy?
    A. Roman violations of border agreements with Carthage
    B. Rome's banishing Carthage from the Iberus
    C. revenge upon the Roman general for defeating Hannibal in Spain
    D. Roman dictation of Carthage's friends and enemies

10. If the passage were to be outlined as four parts, which of the following parts would not belong?
    F. sympathize with enemy's objective
    G. deride enemy's abilities
    H. show confidence in troops
    J. identify misdeeds of enemy

Level Nine

Vocabulary
Power Plus
for the
ACT
Vocabulary,
Reading, and Writing
Exercises for High Scores

Lesson Five

1. **jaded** (jā´ did) *adj.* worn out; dulled, as from overindulgence
   Kate became *jaded* about love after the third boyfriend in a month broke up with her.
   syn: exhausted; wearied   *ant: fresh*

2. **gist** (jist) *n.* the main point
   I never did understand the *gist* of his story.
   syn: idea; essence

3. **advocate** (ad´ və kāt) *v.* to recommend; to speak in favor of
   The neutral organization does not *advocate* support of a particular candidate or position.
   syn: promote; encourage   *ant: oppose; contest*

4. **efface** (i fās´) *v.* to obliterate; to wipe out
   He tried to *efface* his memories of her by burning all her pictures.
   syn: erase   *ant: enshrine*

5. **charisma** (kə riz´ mə) *n.* personal appeal or attraction; magnetism
   The candidate had *charisma* and good looks, but little knowledge of important issues.
   syn: charm

6. **ogre** (ō´ gər) *n.* a brute; a large monster; a frightful giant
   The *ogre* occasionally emerged from his mountain cave and terrorized the villagers.

7. **mesmerize** (mez´ mə rīz) *v.* to hypnotize
   The fast music and spinning dancers *mesmerized* the audience.
   syn: captivate; entrance   *ant: bore*

8. **entity** (en´ ti tē) *n.* anything having existence, either physical or mystical
   Ann thought that she saw a ghostly *entity* hovering over the graveyard, but it turned out to be a flag blowing in the wind.

9. **bandy** (ban´ dē) *v.* to exchange words; to discuss casually
   Let's not *bandy* words about the deal any more; just sign the papers and leave, please.

10. **dastardly** (das´ tərd lē) *adj.* cowardly and treacherous
The *dastardly* thief stole money only from helpless, elderly people.
syn: dishonorable; shameful   *ant: righteous*

Exercise I

Words in Context

From the list below, supply the words needed to complete the paragraph. Some words will not be used.

charisma	efface	ogre	advocate
gist	bandy	mesmerize	

1. Joan, who _____ the cleanup of the James River, is always trying to gain supporters for her cause. The usual _____ of her speech focuses on the effects of the river's pollution on future generations. Her eloquent speech _____ audiences, and her _____ helps her to win the hearts of people who are not even affected by the James River. Joan hopes that her efforts will someday help to _____ the irresponsible dumping practices that continue to foul the James River.

From the list below, supply the words needed to complete the paragraph. Some words will not be used.

dastardly	gist	entity	jaded
ogre	bandy	charisma	

2. The _____ athlete, accustomed to winning first place, wanted to be happy with her third-place trophy, but deep down, she felt that months of intensive training had gone to waste. On the bus ride home, she refused to _____ compliments or even joke about the race with her teammates. She could think only about the _____ runner who intentionally tripped her early in the race and likely cost her the win. Myra thought, "This unsportsmanlike _____ should not be allowed to compete in track meets. Myra didn't see the other girl after the race, but merely thinking of that horrid _____ would haunt Myra for weeks to come.

Exercise II

Sentence Completion

Complete the sentence in a way that shows you understand the meaning of the italicized vocabulary word.

1. Sally described enough of the movie for Bill to get the *gist* of it, but not enough to…

2. The jury was shocked when, during the trial, the *dastardly* criminal…

3. Mom would not *bandy* any comments about extending my curfew because she felt that…

4. The *jaded* artist decided to find a new career when…

5. The revolutionaries *effaced* statues of the former dictator because…

6. Mondello the Great *mesmerized* the children at the birthday party by…

7. Someone who *advocates* good manners might become angry if you…

8. The overwhelming *charisma* of the cult leader made it easy for him to…

9. The linebackers on the football team looked like *ogres* compared to…

10. Mom had to explain to Maggie that an imaginary friend is not a real *entity*; it is…

Exercise III

Roots, Prefixes, and Suffixes

Study the entries and answer the questions that follow.

The root *fort* means "strong."
The root *graph* means "writing."
The root *gen* means "born," "to produce," or "kind" (type).
The prefix *mono* means "one."

1. *Using literal translations as guidance, define the following words without using a dictionary.*

   A. generic   D. fort
   B. generate   E. monologue
   C. fortify   F. graphic

2. The coach says that this year, the strong players on the team have the _____ to make it to the championships. The activity that you do best—your strong point—might be called your _____.

3. A group of people born within a certain time period is a[n] _____.
   Your _____ will determine what physical traits you will have.

4. List all the words that you can think of that contain the roots *graph* and *gen*.

Exercise IV

Inference

Complete the sentences by inferring information about the italicized word from its context.

1. If you didn't understand the *gist* of the lecture, then you should find the teacher after class and ask...

2. When someone who *advocates* energy conservation sees lights left on, he or she might...

3. If you *efface* your fears about flying, then you might be willing to...

Exercise V

Writing

Here is a writing prompt similar to the one you will find on the essay writing portion of the ACT.

> The United States presently enjoys an all-volunteer military, meaning that no one is forced into service or combat; however, several Western nations presently enforce mandatory military or government service for all citizens (conscription).
>
> Proponents of conscription claim that mandatory service for everyone will galvanize public awareness of news and politics because every person will have a direct stake in what the military or government must do—especially in the context of engaging in war. Opponents rebut the idea that conscription actually changes anything about the way in which nations go to war, citing unpopular wars in history that occurred when military service was indeed mandatory.
>
> Should every citizen of a free nation be forced to participate in the government or military, beyond simply voting for representatives, in order to enjoy the rights specified in the constitution? Argue your position and support your argument with at least three subtopics based on your observations, reading, or experiences.

Thesis: Write a *one-sentence* response to the above assignment. Make certain this single sentence offers a clear statement of your position.

Example: State service, either military or civilian, should be mandatory for anyone who wishes to receive the benefits of the nation.

_____

_____

Organizational Plan: List at least three subtopics you will use to support your main idea. This list is your outline.

1. _____

2. _____

3. _____

Draft: Following your outline, write a good first draft of your essay. Remember to support all your points with examples, facts, references to reading, etc.

Review and Revise: Exchange essays with a classmate. Using the scoring guide for Sentence Formation and Variety on page 219, score your partner's essay (while he or she scores yours). Focus on sentence structure and use of language conventions. If necessary, rewrite your essay to improve the sentence structure and/or your use of language.

Exercise VI

English Practice

Identifying Sentence Errors

Identify the errors in the following sentences. Choose the answer that fixes the error. If the sentence contains no error, select NO CHANGE.

1. Larry said that he had personally designed the web pages <u>with the help of himself and</u> his employees.
    A. NO CHANGE
    B. with his own help and
    C. with help from
    D. with him and

2. <u>I didn't do nothing</u> for the last ten minutes but argue with my sister.
    F. NO CHANGE
    G. I did not do nothing
    H. I did do nothing
    J. I didn't do anything

3. Problems with aggressive <u>wildlife often begins</u> with aggressive human beings.
    A. NO CHANGE
    B. wildlife often begin
    C. wildlife, often begin,
    D. wildlife begins, often,

4. The <u>patients</u> in the front room were given their flu shots.
    F. NO CHANGE
    G. patience
    H. patient's
    J. patients'

5. Proponents for the construction of a new intrastate expressway <u>includes</u> at least four people known to be affiliated with organized crime operations.
    A. NO CHANGE
    B. including
    C. includes:
    D. include

Improving Sentences

The underlined portion of each sentence below contains some flaw. Select the answer that best corrects the flaw.

6. The victims were lying on the ground and firemen arrived to douse the flames and take them to the hospital.
    F. Fireman arrived to douse the flames and take the victims lying on the ground to the hospital.
    G. After dousing the flames on the ground, the firemen took the victims to the hospital.
    H. Firemen arrived to douse the flames, when victims were lying on the ground, and they were taken to the hospital.
    J. Victims lying on the ground were taken to the hospital and firemen arrived to douse the flames.

7. Because of the hurricane warning, everyone sat inside and talked about the game around the dining room table.
    A. sat inside, around the dining room table, and talked about the game.
    B. sat inside and talked around the dining room table.
    C. talked and sat inside about the game, around the dining room table.
    D. talked about the game inside, around the dining room table.

8. We intend to measure the individual results against its costs.
    F. against the costs.
    G. against costs.
    H. against their costs.
    J. with their costs.

9. Deep-sea fishing no longer fascinates me as much as to go to computer demonstrations.
    A. I am interested in computer demonstrations.
    B. going to computer demonstrations.
    C. to go to a computer demonstration.
    D. computer demonstrations.

10. Amadeus Mozart was a brilliant composer he was said to be a perfectionist too.
    F. Mozart was said to be a perfectionist and he was a brilliant composer.
    G. A brilliant composer, Mozart was said to be a perfectionist.
    H. Although he was said to be a perfectionist, Mozart was a brilliant composer
    J. A brilliant composer, although a perfectionist, was said to be Mozart.

Level Nine

Vocabulary
Power Plus
for the ACT
Vocabulary,
Reading, and Writing
Exercises for High Scores

Lesson Six

1. **nepotism** (nep´ ə tiz əm) *n.* favoritism shown to family or friends
   by those in power, especially in business or hiring practices
   I was qualified for the job, but Uncle Mike refused to hire me because he
   did not want to be accused of *nepotism*.

2. **begrudge** (bi gruj´) *v.* to resent another's success; to envy
   Craig, the younger brother, secretly *begrudged* Brian's fortune.
   syn: resent   *ant: forgive*

3. **mandarin** (man´ də rin) *n.* an influential person; a member of an elite
   group
   Mandarins and bureaucrats discussed the state of the economy during the
   summit.

4. **glutinous** (glōōt´ n əs) *adj.* gluey; sticky
   The bread dough was in a *glutinous* mass that stuck to anything it touched.

5. **enmity** (en´ mi tē) *n.* deep-seated hostility, often mutual
   Angry stares revealed the mutual *enmity* between Steve and his supervisor.
   syn: hatred; antagonism   *ant: friendship*

6. **declaim** (di klām´) *v.* to speak in a dramatic, impassioned, or
   blustering manner
   At the debate, each politician *declaimed* against the policies of the others.
   syn: trumpet   *ant: whisper*

7. **imbue** (im byōō´) *v.* to inspire or influence; to saturate
   Her hard-working mother *imbued* Jane with a solid work ethic.
   syn: instill; pervade

8. **gaff** (gaf) *n.* a pole with a large hook on one end
   The fisherman used a *gaff* to drag the heavy swordfish onto the boat.

9. **quaff** (kwof) *v.* to drink in large quantities; to gulp
   The old captain *quaffed* his ale and then ordered another stein.
   syn: guzzle; swig   *ant: sip*

10. **bibliophile** (bib´ lē ə fīl) *n.* a lover of books
    The *bibliophile* was thrilled to get a job at the library.

Exercise I

Words in Context

From the list below, supply the words needed to complete the paragraph. Some words will not be used.

nepotism   declaim   imbue   begrudged   enmity

1. The _____ between Mike and Brad showed through the manner in which they argued over the most trivial company decisions. Weeks before, Brad had been promoted to regional manager in an obvious act of _____, since his uncle is a member of the board of directors. Mike _____ Brad for the promotion because it had taken fifteen years for Mike to become a regional manager, and Brad had walked into the job with practically no experience at all. Now, during any argument with Brad, Mike was sure to _____ about how "fifteen years of seniority and experience make my decisions practically infallible."

From the list below, supply the words needed to complete the paragraph. Some words will not be used.

nepotism   mandarin   bibliophile   imbue

2. Corporate leaders, high-ranking government officials, and influential _____ gathered in the halls of Xavier's mansion at least once a month. Dinner was held in the ballroom, and then Xavier, a noted _____, usually invited his guests to his colossal private library. Bookshelves towered over the guests, and the presence of hundreds of rare, ancient tomes _____ them with a sense of humility as they stood among the centuries of human thought that had built the world in which they now lived.

From the list below, supply the words needed to complete the paragraph. Some words will not be used.

glutinous   **quaff**   **declaim**   **gaff**

3. When the whaling ship encountered a tiny skiff bobbing on the high seas, the captain ordered a sailor to snag it with a[n] _____. To the sailor's surprise, a sun-beaten man lay on the bottom of the boat. He awoke to the voices of his rescuers, and he immediately _____ the water they offered him. Apparently, the man had kept himself alive by eating the _____ remnants of wet rations that he salvaged before a violent storm sunk his ship.

Exercise II

Sentence Completion

Complete the sentence in a way that shows you understand the meaning of the italicized vocabulary word.

1. During a break from toiling in the oppressive heat, the workers *quaffed*...

2. Dad spent all day fixing the car and then *declaimed* that...

3. The man working in the reptile exhibit used a *gaff* to...

4. Some parents accused the coach of *nepotism* because...

5. Working on a farm *imbued* Mary with...

6. The activists wanted Dorian's support because he is a *mandarin* who can...

7. You knew that Frank was a *bibliophile* because...

8. The scientist said that the *glutinous* substance had similar characteristics to...

9. There was *enmity* between the brother and sister ever since...

10. Gloria secretly *begrudged* her friend...

Exercise III

Roots, Prefixes, and Suffixes

Study the entries and answer the questions that follow.

The prefix *biblio* means "book."
The root *mort* means "death."
The roots *voc* and *vok* mean "to call."

1. *Using literal translations as guidance, define the following words without using a dictionary.*

    A. bibliography   D. vocation
    B. biblical   E. vociferous
    C. mortician   F. mortuary

2. If you get too many speeding tickets, the department of transportation might call back, or _____, your driver's license. An *advocate* is someone who _____ a particular cause.

3. List as many words as you can think of that contain the roots *mort*, *voc*, and *vok*.

Exercise IV

Inference

Complete the sentences by inferring information about the italicized word from its context.

1. *Nepotism* is common in family businesses, where many of the employees are hired because they...

2. Kelly attributed her artistic success to the fact that her mentor had *imbued* her with...

3. If people avoid you because you always *declaim* your own skills, then you should probably learn to...

Exercise V

Critical Reading

Below is a reading passage followed by several multiple-choice questions similar to the ones you will encounter on the ACT. Carefully read the passage and choose the best answer for each of the questions.

The following passage is an adaptation of a letter written in 1904 by President Theodore Roosevelt. Roosevelt is remembered for his limitless energy, his aggressive foreign and domestic policies, his economic reform, and his often-militant patriotic fervor. The passage reveals a side of Roosevelt of which many citizens were unaware.

Dear Ted:

This will be a long business letter. I sent to you the examination papers for West Point and Annapolis. I have thought a great deal over the matter, and discussed it at great length with Mother. I feel on the one hand that I ought to give you my best advice, and yet on the other hand I do not wish to seem to constrain you
5   against your wishes. If you have definitely made up your mind that you have an overmastering desire to be in the Navy or the Army, and that such a career is the one in which you will take a really heart-felt interest—far more so than any other—and that your greatest chance for happiness and usefulness will lie in doing this one work to which you feel yourself especially drawn—why, under such circumstances,
10   I have but little to say. But I am not satisfied that this is really your feeling. It seemed to me more as if you did not feel drawn in any other direction, and wondered what you were going to do in life or what kind of work you would turn your hand to, and wondered if you could make a success or not; and that you are therefore inclined to turn to the Navy or Army chiefly because you would then have a definite and settled
15   career in life, and could hope to go on steadily without any great risk of failure. Now, if such is your thought, I shall quote to you what Captain Mahan said of his son when asked why he did not send him to West Point or Annapolis. "I have too much confidence in him to make me feel that it is desirable for him to enter either branch of the service."
20   I have great confidence in you. I believe you have the ability and, above all, the energy, the perseverance, and the common sense, to win out in civil life. That you will have some hard times and some discouraging times I have no question; but this is merely another way of saying that you will share the common lot. Though you will have to work in different ways from those in which I worked, you will not
25   have to work any harder, nor to face periods of more discouragement. I trust in your ability, and especially your character, and I am confident you will win.
In the Army and the Navy the chance for a man to show great ability and rise above his fellows does not occur on the average more than once in a generation. When I was down at Santiago it was melancholy for me to see how fossilized and
30   lacking in ambition, and generally useless, were most of the men of my age and over, who had served their lives in the Army. The Navy for the last few years has

been better, but for twenty years after the Civil War there was less chance in the
Navy than in the Army to practice, and do, work of real consequence. I have actually
known lieutenants in both the Army and the Navy who were grandfathers—men
35 who had seen their children married before they themselves attained the grade of
captain. Of course the chance may come at any time when the man of West Point
or Annapolis who will have stayed in the Army or Navy finds a great war on, and
therefore has the opportunity to rise high. Under such circumstances, I think that
the man of such training who has actually left the Army or the Navy has even more
40 chance of rising than the man who has remained in it. Moreover, often a man can
do as I did in the Spanish War, even though not a West-Pointer. This last point
raises the question about you going to West Point or Annapolis and leaving the
Army or Navy after you have served the regulation four years (I think that is the
number) after graduation from the academy. Under this plan you would have an
45 excellent education and a grounding in discipline and, in some ways, a testing of
your capacity greater than I think you can get in any ordinary college. On the other
hand, except for the profession of an engineer, you would have had nothing like
special training, and you would be so ordered about, and arranged for, that you
would have less independence of character than you could gain from them. You
50 would have had fewer temptations; but you would have had less chance to develop
the qualities which overcome temptations and show that a man has individual
initiative. Supposing you entered at seventeen, with the intention of following
this course. The result would be that at twenty-five you would leave the Army or
Navy without having gone through any law school or any special technical school
55 of any kind, and would start your life work three or four years later than your
schoolfellows of today, who go to work immediately after leaving college. Of course,
under such circumstances, you might study law, for instance, during the four years
after graduation; but my own feeling is that a man does good work chiefly when he
is in something which he intends to make his permanent work, and in which he
60 is deeply interested. Moreover, there will always be the chance that the number of
officers in the Army or Navy will be deficient, and that you would have to stay in
the service instead of getting out when you wished.

   I want you to think over all these matters very seriously. It would be a great
misfortune for you to start into the Army or Navy as a career, and find that you
65 had mistaken your desires and had gone in without really weighing the matter. You
ought not to enter unless you feel genuinely drawn to the life as a life-work. If so,
go in; but not otherwise.

   Mr. Loeb told me today that at seventeen he had tried for the army, but failed.
The competitor who beat him in is now a captain; Mr. Loeb has passed him by,
70 although meanwhile a war has been fought. Mr. Loeb says he wished to enter the
army because he did not know what to do, could not foresee whether he would
succeed or fail in life, and felt the army would give him "a living and a career."
Now if this is at bottom your feeling I should advise you not to go in; I should say
yes to some boys, but not to you; I believe in you too much, and have too much
75 confidence in you.

1. The letter is
    A. a summary of Roosevelt's thoughts about the military.
    B. a list of reasons to join the military.
    C. advice about a permanent career, outside of the military.
    D. a set of considerations about whether to pursue a military career.

2. Which of the following best describes the purpose of the passage?
    F. describe
    G. analyze
    H. persuade
    J. inform

3. According to the author, Ted wants to attend military school because
    A. he knows that the military will provide opportunities for success.
    B. he doesn't know what he wants to do, but he wants a steady career.
    C. he wants a steady career that offers more excitement than college.
    D. Captain Mahan told Ted that he would have potential as an officer.

4. According to the author of the passage, participating in a war is
    F. detrimental, because of the risk.
    G. an opportunity to succeed.
    H. character-building, because it provides better challenges than college.
    J. good for professional soldiers, but not sailors.

5. Which of the following is *not* a reason why a military education followed
    by a short career would be beneficial?
    A. The military helps to develop discipline.
    B. Military schools provide excellent educations.
    C. The military would prepare a student for a political career.
    D. A military engineer would have the special training for a civilian career.

6. Which best paraphrases what the author says in lines 59-61?

    > "...my own feeling is that a man does good work chiefly when he is
    > in something which he intends to make his permanent work, and in
    > which he is deeply interested."

    F. People who do not choose the right career just have to learn to deal
       with it.
    G. Decide what you want to do before committing your life to a career.
    H. Choose your career based on what you want to do for the rest of
       your life.
    J. People do their best work when they love what they are doing.

7. As used in line 61, *deficient* most nearly means
   A. lacking.
   B. deployed.
   C. captured.
   D. improper.

8. According to the passage, the existence of temptation is
   F. dangerous because it can lead to imprisonment in the military.
   G. good because it provokes thought.
   H. necessary because it separates the good from the bad.
   J. good because it inspires resistance and individuality.

9. Mr. Loeb was Roosevelt's advisor. The mention of Loeb's story in the final paragraph suggests which of the following?
   A. People can achieve as much success as civilians as they can as members of the military.
   B. Loeb was lucky to become a presidential advisor.
   C. People should enlist in the Navy, not the Army.
   D. People who do not make Captain should get leave the Army because they can have better civilian careers.

10. The tone of this passage is best described as
    F. anxious and judgmental.
    G. panicked and bossy.
    H. concerned and supportive.
    J. pleased and affectionate.

Lesson Seven

1. **gird** (gûrd) *v.* to prepare for an event or an action
   Residents of the shore *girded* themselves for the upcoming hurricane.
   syn: brace

2. **daunt** (dônt) *v.* to make afraid; to discourage
   The high waves and the approaching storm did not *daunt* the treasure hunters.
   syn: intimidate; dishearten   *ant: encourage*

3. **flux** (fluks) *n.* a state of continual change or movement
   The constant *flux* of the stock market now makes investing risky.
   syn: fluctuation; instability   *ant: stability; solidity*

4. **hovel** (hov´əl) *n.* a wretched living place; an open shed
   The child welfare agent removed the children from the filthy *hovel*.
   syn: shanty; shack   *ant: palace; mansion*

5. **cadaverous** (kə dav´ ər əs) *adj.* of or like a corpse; pale, gaunt, thin
   The old pirate's *cadaverous* face made the young sailor tremble.
   syn: ghastly   *ant: robust; healthy*

6. **gothic** (goth´ ik) *adj.* of the middle ages; of or relating to a
   mysterious, grotesque, and desolate style of fiction
   A romantic story line offset some of the dreary and gloomy elements of the *gothic* novel.

7. **penury** (pen´ yə rē) *n.* extreme poverty
   Though born into *penury*, he became one of the country's wealthiest entrepreneurs.
   syn: destitution   *ant: wealth; opulence*

8. **egress** (ē´ gres) *n.* an exit; a means of going out
   The only *egress* on the submarine was the main hatch on the tower.
   syn: passage   *ant: ingress; entrance*

9. **felicity** (fə lis´ i tē) *n.* happiness; bliss
Rose mistakenly thought that her wealth ensured *felicity*, but she quickly learned that money does not buy happiness.
syn: euphoria; delight   *ant: unhappiness; discontent*

10. **despot** (des´ pət) *n.* a dictator with absolute power
During his rule, Stalin was a despot responsible for the death of millions of his own people.

Exercise I

Words in Context

From the list below, supply the words needed to complete the paragraph. Some words will not be used.

flux	hovel	despot	gird
egress	cadaverous	penury	

1. When the prince assassinated his father the monarch, and seized control of the government, the already poor nation became one of abject _____.
The majority of citizens lived in poorly maintained _____ that would likely be condemned by the standards of most other nations. Starvation and epidemics turned what should have been healthy, young workers into _____ zombies who hoped to have enough energy to scrounge for roots to feed their families. Citizens had only two means of _____ from the misery—through the demilitarized zone or across the border into China. Escape was a risky undertaking; if captured, refugees faced imprisonment or execution, on orders from the new _____.

From the list below, supply the words needed to complete the paragraph. Some words will not be used.

felicity	penury	gird	flux
daunt	gothic	hovel	

2. Despite their tremendous destructive power, tornadoes do not _____ the Russell family; they have experienced too many storms even to care. The weather conditions of the Midwest are in constant _____, and the family seldom allows adverse weather to detract from the _____ of their day-to-day lives. Their underground shelter might resemble a[n] _____ dungeon, but for the Russells, it is a place to sit out the storm and listen to Mr. Russell's stories about how he weathered storms during his childhood. He often relates the day in which a tornado passed while he was far from shelter, and he and his parents _____ themselves for the oncoming storm.

Exercise II

Sentence Completion

Complete the sentence in a way that shows you understand the meaning of the italicized vocabulary word.

1. The family lived a life of *penury* after…

2. The children exhibited total *felicity* while…

3. The *gothic* architecture of the castle is characteristic of…

4. Don't let the size of the players *daunt* you; they're not…

5. Linda *girded* herself against the swarm of killer bees by…

6. When Connie saw the *cadaverous* refugees, she immediately…

7. The wealthy industrialist was born in a *hovel*, but he…

8. If Amy had not found an *egress* from the burning house, she…

9. Because of the *flux* of customers, Sal didn't know if her restaurant would…

10. The *despot* ordered his guards to…

Exercise III

Roots, Prefixes, and Suffixes

Study the entries and answer the questions that follow.

The suffix *ism* means "belief in."
The root *deci* means "ten."
The prefix *anti* means "against."
The roots *duc* and *duct* mean "to lead."
The root *do* means "to give."

1. *Using literal translations as guidance, define the following words without using a dictionary.*

    A. idealism   D. objectivism
    B. abduct   E. duct
    C. donate   F. pardon

2. A medicine that works against certain symptoms by taking them away is called a[n] _____. A battleship might have _____ guns for use against enemy planes.

3. A[n] _____ is a ten-year period, and the word that originally meant "to kill every tenth person" is _____.

4. List as many words as you can think of that contain the roots *duc* or *duct*.

Exercise IV

Inference

Complete the sentences by inferring information about the italicized word from its context.

1. In order to elicit a confession, a detective might try to *daunt* an overconfident suspect by...

2. A homeless person living in *penury* would probably appreciate...

3. If a city experiences a *flux* in population, then people are...

Exercise V

Writing

Here is a writing prompt similar to the one you will find on the essay writing portion of the ACT.

> Building a nation is a centuries-long process, but it begins with a solid foundation of rules and rights that will influence or dictate the nation's growth, shape, and political dynamics.
>
> Imagine that you have just founded your very own nation in a geographic region of your choosing. The first order of business, and your assignment, is to write a constitution, or a charter, that details what your government can and cannot do in your nation (a lawless dictatorship is not an option). Your first constitution will deal with generalities such as rights—not specific laws on personal behavior.
>
> Think of the top three principles that you would include in your constitution and explain why each one is necessary and important. Your points should be specific, e.g., no "everyone will be nice to each other." Remember to include an introduction and conclusion to your argument. Support your topic with examples, stories, or your own ideas and observations. Be sure to explain why each of your subtopics is essential to your nation, and how, or if, they are linked to one another.

Thesis: Write a *one-sentence* response to the above assignment. Make certain this single sentence offers a clear statement of your position.

> *Example: The three main rights of citizens in my nation will be based on the idea that no one will be forced to pay for or participate in services they do not want or need.*

_____

_____

Organizational Plan: List at least three subtopics you will use to support your main idea. This list is your outline.

1. _____

2. _____

3. _____

Draft: Following your outline, write a good first draft of your essay. Remember to support all your points with examples, facts, references to reading, etc.

Review and Revise: Exchange essays with a classmate. Use the scoring guide for Word Choice on page 220 to score your partner's essay (while he or she scores yours). Focus on the word choice and use of language conventions. If necessary, rewrite your essay to improve the word choice and/or your use of language.

Exercise VI

English Practice

Improving Paragraphs
Read the following passage and then choose the best revision for the underlined portions of the paragraph. The questions will require you to make decisions regarding the revision of the reading selection. Some revisions are not of actual mistakes, but will improve the clarity of the writing.

[1]

(1) Plaid may not be exactly what you think it is. (2) Tartan may be <u>which</u>[1] you think plaid is.

    1. A. NO CHANGE
       B. that
       C. witch
       D. what

[2]

(3) Autumn usually finds us wrapped in a tartan, whether they are around our torsos, <u>are</u>[2] legs, or a combination of both. (4) The use of a <u>"plaid"</u>[3] seems to come into fashion every autumn and can be a handsome addition to any outfit. (5) Warmth is a bonus of wearing a plaid, no matter what design it is.

    2. F. NO CHANGE   3. A. NO CHANGE
       G. ore   B. plaid
       H. our   C. plaid"
       J. hour   D. 'plaid'

4. Which of the following describes
   the error in sentence 3?
   F. run-on sentence
   G. sentence fragment
   H. improper pronoun
      agreement
   J. incorrect prepositional
      phrase

[3]

(6) A plaid, you see, is a <u>woven piece</u>[5] of fabric worn over the shoulder or sometimes tucked under a belt to hold it in place. (7) <u>The designs</u>[6] of various colored stripes crossing at right angles is rightfully a tartan; many a plaid is a tartan design.

5.	A. NO CHANGE	6.	F. NO CHANGE
	B. woven, piece,		G. The design
	C. woven; piece		H. The design's
	D. woven peace		J. The design,

[4]

(8) <u>Autumn is a great time</u>[7] of the year to purchase a <u>favorite tartan, and sew</u>[8] a lovely, long skirt for informal entertaining at home. (9) The closet must be full of soft old shirts of particular tartans to wrap around our shoulders for a quick trip to the post office. (10) The design is an old <u>favorite, for ties; and scarves; lap robes, and carriage covers</u>[9] for baby's stroller. (11) Some believe that the tartan design <u>was began</u>[10] as a way to incorporate expensive, dyed threads in cheap materials. (12) No matter what you choose to tailor, it is guaranteed to be an eye-catching, original design.

7. A. NO CHANGE
   B. autumn: it is a great time
   C. autumn, it is a great time
   D. autumn; is a great time

8. F. NO CHANGE
   G. tartan, sew
   H. tartan and sew
   J. tartan; and sew

9. A. NO CHANGE
   B. favorite for ties and scarves
      lap robes, and carriage
      covers
   C. favorite for ties, and scarves,
      lap robes, and carriage
      covers
   D. favorite for ties and scarves,
      lap robes, and carriage
      covers

10.F. NO CHANGE
    G. begun
    H. originated
    J. was original

11. Which sentence should be
    deleted from paragraph 4?
    A. sentence 8
    B. sentence 9
    C. sentence 10
    D. sentence 11

[5]

(13) If you have a yen for pretty colors and patterns with classic lines, feel free to make yourself a plaid with knotted tassels on the edge. (14) Wear it for warmth and style as you enjoy the autumn weather. (15) If you have a fear of tying, <u>then buy</u>[12] a huge tartan scarf and throw it over <u>you're</u>[13] shoulder with a flair for flamboyance.

12.F. NO CHANGE
    G. than buy
    H. however buy
    J. because you can buy

13.A. NO CHANGE
    B. over you' are
    C. over yore
    D. over your

14. Which of the following suggestions would improve the development of the beginning of the passage?
    F. Exchange paragraphs 1 and 3.
    G. Exchange paragraphs 2 and 3.
    H. Exchange paragraphs 3 and 1.
    J. Exchange paragraphs 1 and 2.

15. Which of the following changes would best improve the concluding paragraph?
    A. Reverse the order of the sentences.
    B. Exchange sentences 13 and 14.
    C. Exchange sentences 14 and 15.
    D. Delete the paragraph.

Vocabulary
Power Plus
for the ACT
Vocabulary,
Reading, and Writing
Exercises for High Scores

REVIEW
Lessons 1–7

Exercise I

Sentence Completion

Choose the best pair of words to complete the sentence. Most choices will fit grammatically and will even make sense logically, but you must choose the pair that best fits the idea of the sentence.

1. The dictator of the poor nation hosted _____ banquets for international guests, hoping to distract them from the _____ of the starving population in the ghettos and fields beyond the palace walls.
    A. dastardly, fealty
    B. ostentatious, penury
    C. belated, nepotism
    D. cadaverous, paucity
    E. egalitarian, enmity

2. The rampant _____ within the company _____ good workers who, unlike cousins of the owner, could be fired for doing poor work.
    A. gist, gorges
    B. edifice, girds
    C. blight, daunts
    D. nepotism, alienates
    E. despot, bilks

3. Each generation prolonged the longstanding _____ between the nations by fostering the _____ belief that the enemy would inevitably invade and plunder the other's resources.
    A. opiate, laggard
    B. egress, pensive
    C. enmity, fatalistic
    D. gaff, berserk
    E. epigram, fallow

4. It took Derek a few weeks to get used to the _____ plumbing while living in the _____ his miserly uncle built from scraps from the lumber yard.
   A. dastardly, flux
   B. felonious, paucity
   C. glutinous, edifice
   D. antiquated, hovel
   E. licentious, denizen

5. The con artist _____ the _____ with the prospect of purchasing an extremely rare double-eagle quarter.
   A. enticed, numismatist
   B. alienated, ogre
   C. dallied, mandarin
   D. eluded, blight
   E. kneaded, bibliophile

6. After enjoying a few years of absolute power, the _____ began to _____ himself into thinking that he was the savior of his nation.
   A. caricature, daunt
   B. despot, delude
   C. ogre, gorge
   D. mandarin, animate
   E. gaff, gratify

7. Having read thousands of books, the _____ could usually guess the _____ of a commercial novel after reading only the first chapter or two.
   A. mandarin, flux
   B. charisma, enmity
   C. numismatist, paucity
   D. denizen, entity
   E. bibliophile, gist

8. Television hurts the _____ aspect of democratic elections because candidates who demonstrate _____ or good looks tend to beat candidates who lack those characteristics, regardless of intellect.
   A. egalitarian, charisma
   B. ambidextrous, penury
   C. ostentatious, egress
   D. lackadaisical, felicity
   E. laggard, paucity

Exercise II

Crossword Puzzle

Use the clues to complete the crossword puzzle. The answers consist of vocabulary words from lessons 1 through 7.

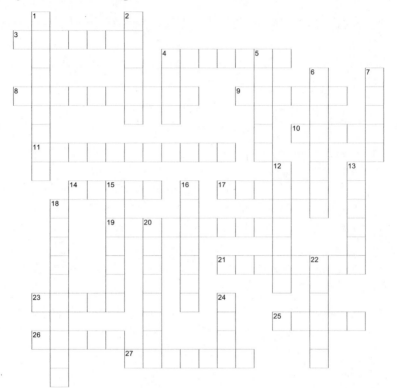

Across

3. occupant; inhabitant
4. to please
8. an exaggerated portrayal
9. in high spirits
10. dirty, wretched living place
11. promoting equal rights
14. to inspire or influence
17. exit; means of going out
19. morally unrestrained
21. to resent another's success
23. worn out; dulled
25. to escape notice
26. to make afraid; to discourage
27. scarcity; lack

Down

1. to besiege by encircling
2. deep-seated hostility
4. to prepare for an event
5. inactive; unproductive
6. favoritism shown to family or friends
7. to waste time
12. in a state of violent rage
13. to wipe out
15. delayed
16. dreamily thoughtful
18. to combine
20. personal appeal; magnetism
22. to mislead; to fool
24. main point

Level Nine

**Vocabulary
Power Plus**
for the
ACT Vocabulary,
Reading, and Writing
Exercises for High Scores

Lesson Eight

1. **beget** (bi get´) *v.* to produce; to make happen
   Hatred merely *begets* more hatred.
   syn: generate   *ant: prevent*

2. **educe** (i dōōs´) *v.* to draw or bring out
   The lawyer tried to *educe* a response from the witness.
   syn: elicit   *ant: suppress*

3. **glean** (glēn) *v.* to collect bit by bit; to gather with patient labor
   The investigator *gleaned* pertinent information from the witnesses to the crash.
   syn: garner   *ant: disperse*

4. **chafe** (chāf) *v.* to wear or irritate, often through rubbing or friction
   The freezing wind *chafed* our faces as we struggled through the storm.

5. **effrontery** (i frun´ tə rē) *n.* shameless boldness
   The thief had the *effrontery* to demand a reward for returning the credit
   cards he had stolen.
   syn: impudence; nerve; audacity   *ant: timidity*

6. **imbibe** (im bīb´) *v.* to drink (especially alcohol)
   After the raid, the Vikings feasted and *imbibed* to the point of physical
   sickness.

7. **feign** (fān) *v.* to pretend
   He *feigned* an interest in the conversation, but his mind wandered elsewhere.
   syn: simulate; fake

8. **desist** (di sist´) *v.* to stop; discontinue
   The police ordered the rioters to immediately *desist* from further protests.
   syn: cease; end   *ant: begin; start*

9. **allude** (ə lōōd´) *v.* to hint at, to refer to indirectly
   The attorney *alluded* to a cover-up without actually mentioning it.
   syn: suggest; imply   *ant: expose*

10. **elite** (e lēt´) *n.* the choice members or best of a group
    Soldiers in the Special Forces are part of the military's *elite*.
    syn: leaders   *ant: common; multitude*

Exercise I

Words in Context

From the list below, supply the words needed to complete the paragraph. Some words will not be used.

beget	imbibe	chafe	feign
desist	glean	effrontery	educe

1. Kate had had emotional issues all her life, and she knew that one serious problem could easily _____ another. Her psychologist used a form of hypnotism to _____ her patient's childhood memories. Little by little, the doctor _____ clues that might hint at the solution to Kate's disorder. Originally, the doctor worried that Kate would _____ compliance and simply pretend to remember things, but the doctor could tell that the memories were real by the way in which they seemed to _____ the patient emotionally. One hour was all Kate could stand before she had to ask the doctor to _____ for the day.

From the list below, supply the words needed to complete the paragraph. Some words will not be used.

effrontery	beget	elite
imbibe	allude	

2. As usual, the Senator's cocktail party was a gathering of the society _____. Some guests mingled and chatted about politics while they _____ fine wine, but others demonstrated a social _____ by first eating and then criticizing the host's menu selections. The critics never actually said they didn't enjoy the food, of course; they merely _____ to the host's questionable choice of caterer.

Exercise II

Sentence Completion

Complete the sentence in a way that shows you understand the meaning of the italicized vocabulary word.

1. The councilman was concerned that a pool hall would *beget*...

2. Members of the school's academic *elite* were chosen to...

3. From her moving story, the author hoped that readers would *educe*...

4. Without actually saying what was wrong with the program, Beth *alluded* to...

5. Jaime *gleaned* as much information about painting as she could before she...

6. The teacher told the students that if they didn't *desist*, they would...

7. The criminal complained that his handcuffs *chafed*...

8. Neil *feigned* sickness in an effort to...

9. In a display of *effrontery*, the waiter...

10. The festive bunch feasted and *imbibed* after...

Roots, Prefixes, and Suffixes

Study the entries and answer the questions that follow.

The root *termin* means "end" or "boundary."
The root *ver* means "true."
The roots *dem* and *demos* mean "people."

1. *Using literal translations as guidance, define the following words without using a dictionary.*

   A. terminal   D. verify
   B. terminate   E. verdict
   C. exterminate   F. democracy

2. When many people contract a disease, it is said to be a[n] _____. If *gogue* means "to lead," then a *demagogue* is _____.

3. List as many words as you can think of that contain the root *term*.

Inference

Complete the sentences by inferring information about the italicized word from its context.

1. If someone *feigns* sleep, then he or she...

2. Someone who is afraid to tell you something might instead *allude* to...

3. If the school wants a particular activity to *desist*, it must want...

Exercise V

Critical Reading

Below is a reading passage followed by several multiple-choice questions similar to the ones you will encounter on the ACT. Carefully read the passage and choose the best answer for each of the questions.

The passage is an excerpt from Charles Dickens's Hard Times, *a Victorian novel set in the fictional industrial city of Coketown, England.*

COKETOWN, to which Messrs. Bounderby and Gradgrind now walked, was a triumph of fact; it had no greater taint of fancy in it than Mrs. Gradgrind herself. Let us strike the key-note, Coketown, before pursuing our tune.

It was a town of red brick, or of brick that would have been red if the smoke and
5   ashes had allowed it; but as matters stood, it was a town of unnatural red and black like the painted face of a savage. It was a town of machinery and tall chimneys, out of which interminable serpents of smoke trailed themselves for ever and ever, and never got uncoiled. It had a black canal in it, and a river that ran purple with ill-smelling dye, and vast piles of building full of windows where there was a rattling
10   and a trembling all day long, and where the piston of the steam-engine worked monotonously up and down, like the head of an elephant in a state of melancholy madness. It contained several large streets all very like one another, and many small streets still more like one another, inhabited by people equally like one another, who all went in and out at the same hours, with the same sound upon the same
15   pavements, to do the same work, and to whom every day was the same as yesterday and to-morrow, and every year the counterpart of the last and the next.

These attributes of Coketown were in the main inseparable from the work by which it was sustained; against them were to be set off, comforts of life which found their way all over the world, and elegancies of life which made, we will not ask how
20   much of the fine lady, who could scarcely bear to hear the place mentioned. The rest of its features were voluntary, and they were these.

You saw nothing in Coketown but what was severely workful. If the members of a religious persuasion built a chapel there--as the members of eighteen religious persuasions had done--they made it a pious warehouse of red brick, with sometimes
25   (but this is only in highly ornamental examples) a bell in a birdcage on the top of it. The solitary exception was the New Church; a stuccoed edifice with a square steeple over the door, terminating in four short pinnacles like florid wooden legs. All the public inscriptions in the town were painted alike, in severe characters of black and white. The jail might have been the infirmary, the infirmary might have
30   been the jail, the town-hall might have been either, or both, or anything else, for anything that appeared to the contrary in the graces of their construction. Fact, fact, fact, everywhere in the material aspect of the town; fact, fact, fact, everywhere in the immaterial. The M'Choakumchild school was all fact, and the school of design was all fact, and the relations between master and man were all fact, and everything
35   was fact between the lying-in hospital and the cemetery, and what you couldn't state

in figures, or show to be purchaseable in the cheapest market and saleable in the dearest, was not, and never should be, world without end, Amen.

A town so sacred to fact, and so triumphant in its assertion, of course got on well? Why no, not quite well. No? Dear me!

40 No. Coketown did not come out of its own furnaces, in all respects like gold that had stood the fire. First, the perplexing mystery of the place was, Who belonged to the eighteen denominations? Because, whoever did, the labouring people did not. It was very strange to walk through the streets on a Sunday morning, and note how few of them the barbarous jangling of bells that was driving the sick and

45 nervous mad, called away from their own quarter, from their own close rooms, from the corners of their own streets, where they lounged listlessly, gazing at all the church and chapel going, as at a thing with which they had no manner of concern. Nor was it merely the stranger who noticed this, because there was a native organization in Coketown itself, whose members were to be heard of in the

50 House of Commons every session, indignantly petitioning for acts of parliament that should make these people religious by main force. Then came the Teetotal Society, who complained that these same people would get drunk, and showed in tabular statements that they did get drunk, and proved at tea parties that no inducement, human or Divine (except a medal), would induce them to forego their

55 custom of getting drunk. Then came the chemist and druggist, with other tabular statements, showing that when they didn't get drunk, they took opium. Then came the experienced chaplain of the jail, with more tabular statements, outdoing all the previous tabular statements, and showing that the same people would resort to low haunts, hidden from the public eye, where they heard low singing and saw low

60 dancing, and mayhap joined in it; and where A. B., aged twenty-four next birthday, and committed for eighteen months' solitary, had himself said (not that he had ever shown himself particularly worthy of belief) his ruin began, as he was perfectly sure and confident that otherwise he would have been a tip-top moral specimen. Then came Mr. Gradgrind and Mr. Bounderby, the two gentlemen at this present moment

65 walking through Coketown, and both eminently practical, who could, on occasion, furnish more tabular statements derived from their own personal experience, and illustrated by cases they had known and seen, from which it clearly appeared--in short, it was the only clear thing in the case--that these same people were a bad lot altogether, gentlemen; that do what you would for them they were never thankful

70 for it, gentlemen; that they were restless, gentlemen; that they never knew what they wanted; that they lived upon the best, and bought fresh butter; and insisted on Mocha coffee, and rejected all but prime parts of meat, and yet were eternally dissatisfied and unmanageable. In short, it was the moral of the old nursery fable:

There was an old woman, and what do you think?
75 She lived upon nothing but victuals and drink;
Victuals and drink were the whole of her diet,
And yet this old woman would NEVER be quiet.

1. Overall, the author's portrayal of industry in paragraph 2 is best described as
    A. artful and chaotic.
    B. quiet but optimistic.
    C. diversity and technology.
    D. misery and redundancy.

2. The author probably uses the simile in lines 5-6 to
    F. convey the author's dislike of savages.
    G. imply that savages are employed as plant workers.
    H. describe the way in which the smoke drifts.
    J. contradict the industrial setting with primitive imagery.

3. Choose the most accurate description of the irony in paragraph 3.
    A. The people who purchase the goods made in Coketown are repulsed by the city.
    B. All factory towns look like Coketown, except they are not as polluted.
    C. Even the upper class volunteers to visit Coketown.
    D. Because they are manufactured there, many of life's luxuries are common in Coketown.

4. Which phrase best summarizes the author's portrayal of Coketown's buildings in paragraph 4?
    F. Coketown is a dynamic town with outlets for fine arts and entertainment.
    G. Coketown is orderly—a city of the future.
    H. Coketown itself seems to have been produced in a factory.
    J. Coketown is centered more around religion than industry.

5. Which of the following best paraphrases lines 9-14 of the passage?
    A. The monotonous town had no unique people or characteristics.
    B. Coketown had good days and bad days.
    C. Time passed slowly in the town.
    D. All people enjoyed equal treatment in the town.

6. The "prayer" in line 31-37 suggests that the true religion of Coketown is
    F. a cross between Baptist and Seventh-Day Adventist.
    G. based on fact and production, rather than a deity.
    H. steeped in faith and recovery.
    J. highly imaginative and central to the workers.

7. As used repeatedly in paragraph 6, *tabular* emphasizes
   A. the general good organization of the town.
   B. the overdependency on facts and data.
   C. the similarity between the doctors and the chaplain.
   D. the difference between the government and the laborers.

8. A concerned citizens group of Coketown attempts to convince the government that religion:
   F. should be forced upon the laborers.
   G. is a deeply personal choice and should be ignored.
   H. should be mandatory for workers to receive their paychecks.
   J. needs to be made more appealing to the laborers.

9. As used in line 51-53, *Teetotal Society* probably refers to a group that
   A. sings in a church choir.
   B. drinks heavily, but only in private.
   C. discusses public policy over tea.
   D. attempts to ban alcohol.

10. The tone of the passage is best described as
    F. indifferent.
    G. sardonic.
    H. concerned.
    J. frustrated.

Vocabulary
Power Plus
for the **ACT**
Vocabulary,
Reading, and Writing
Exercises for High Scores

Lesson Nine

1. **bilk**   (bilk)   *v.*   to cheat or swindle; to thwart
   The landscapers tried to *bilk* the homeowner out of money by charging for work that was never authorized.
   syn: defraud; con

2. **homily**   (hom´ ə lē)   *n.*   a sermon
   "Sir," I said, "If I may interrupt you: I need food and clothing for these people, not a *homily* on patience."
   syn: lecture; speech

3. **demise**   (di mīz´)   *n.*   death; a ceasing to exist
   Mary will inherit the estate upon the *demise* of Uncle Irving.
   syn: termination; conclusion

4. **emit**   (i mit´)   *v.*   to send out; to give forth, as in sound or light
   The lamp did not *emit* enough light for reading.
   syn: produce; discharge; release

5. **decadence**   (dek´ ə dəns)   *n.*   moral deterioration
   It is often suggested that Rome fell as a result of its own *decadence*.
   syn: decay; corruption; debauchery   *ant: decency*

6. **aghast**   (ə gast´)   *adj.*   feeling great dismay or horror
   We were *aghast* when we saw the disrespectful manner in which the teenager treated her parents.
   syn: terrified; horrified; shocked

7. **granary**   (gran´ ə rē)   *n.*   a storehouse for grain
   We lost a year's supply of corn when the *granary* burned down.

8. **choleric**   (kol´ ə rik)   *adj.*   easily angered
   He was a *choleric* man, whose temper often got him into trouble.
   syn: irascible; cantankerous   *ant: apathetic; impassive*

9. **impede**   (im pēd´)   *v.*   to hinder, obstruct
   The fan who ran through the outfield *impeded* the progress of the playoff game.
   syn: delay; retard   *ant: aid; encourage*

10. **qualm** (kwäm) *n.* a feeling of uneasiness
    The boy had no *qualms* about cheating on the test.
    syn: misgiving   *ant: ease*

11. **lampoon** (lam pōōn´) *n.* a written satire used to ridicule or attack
    someone
    The *lampoon* of the athletic program in the school newspaper angered the
    players and the coach.
    syn: parody; caricature

12. **narcissistic** (när si sis´ tic) *adj.* conceited; having excessive self-love
    or admiration
    The *narcissistic* criminal cared only about his own fate.
    syn: vain; egotistic   *ant: humble; modest*

13. **eradicate** (i rad´ i kāt) *v.* to wipe out; to destroy
    The pest control specialist *eradicated* the termites in our house.
    syn: eliminate   ant: add; create

14. **fabricate** (fab´ ri kāt) *v.* to concoct; to make up a story in order to
    deceive
    The scientist's career ended when someone discovered that he had
    fabricated his experiments.
    syn: forge; fake

15. **ghastly** (gast´ lē) *adj.* horrible; frightful
    The *ghastly* smile on the dead man at the end of the movie showed that
    he had enjoyed the last laugh.
    syn: dreadful; hideous   *ant: lovely; attractive*

Exercise I

Words in Context

From the list below, supply the words needed to complete the paragraph. Some words will not be used.

decadence	homily	bilk	fabricate
choleric	qualm	narcissistic	

1. The reverend had _____ what he thought was an excellent story for his weekly _____. It was a lengthy parable about a wealthy family that lived in _____ and had no _____ about its lavish lifestyle or mistreatment of servants. The sermon went fairly well until the _____ preacher angrily stopped in mid-sentence to lecture a sleeping member of the congregation.

From the list below, supply the words needed to complete the paragraph. Some words will not be used.

impede	lampoon	demise	granary
ghastly	emit	qualm	

2. Bill arrived at the _____ with his truckload of wheat and with a[n] _____ look on his face. Apparently, the railroad crossing lights had failed to _____ a signal, and Bill had stopped just in time to postpone his _____. The next time he has to drive over railroad tracks, Bill declares, he is going to stop his truck and look both ways, even if he _____ the flow of traffic.

From the list below, supply the words needed to complete the paragraph. Some words will not be used.

narcissistic	decadence	eradicate	bilk
lampoon	aghast	choleric	

3. The author claimed that her article was fiction, but it was actually a[n] _____ that satirized the life of a famous Hollywood figure. It portrayed the famous director as being so _____ that he had mirrors in every room of his mansion so that he could observe his own "perfection" at any given moment. It also portrayed the movie mogul as someone who _____ investors out of their money by knowingly creating box-office failures while pocketing millions. The director was _____ when he read the derisive-but-truthful satire of himself. Within minutes, he was on the phone with his lawyers trying to stop the magazine before the article _____ whatever remained of his credibility.

| **Exercise II** |

Sentence Completion

Complete the sentence in a way that shows you understand the meaning of the italicized vocabulary word.

1. The gauge on the dashboard *emits* a red light when…

2. If the *granary* fills up too early, the farmers will have to…

3. The late night show included *lampoons* meant to…

4. Larry had no *qualms* about…

5. During the *homily*, Jonathan Edwards warned the congregation that…

6. The *demise* of the old West can be attributed to…

7. The *choleric* sailor often found himself in the brig for…

8. *Narcissistic* people seldom worry about…

9. You could tell by the *ghastly* look on her face that she…

10. Some of the games at the carnival are designed to *bilk* people by…

11. You will *impede* the healing of your broken foot if you…

12. *Decadence* among government officials ultimately caused…

13. You will be *aghast* when you see…

14. Dan tried to *eradicate*…

15. Heidi *fabricated* an excuse for…

Exercise III

Roots, Prefixes, and Suffixes

Study the entries and answer the questions that follow.

The root *multi* means "many."
The roots *naut* and *naus* mean "sailor" or "ship."
The roots *nov* and *neo* mean "new."

1. *Using literal translations as guidance, define the following words without using a dictionary.*

   A. innovation   D. multitude
   B. novel   E. multimedia
   C. nautical   F. neoclassical

2. Someone who is new at a sport is said to be a[n] _____. If you restore an old house to new condition, then you _____ it.

3. Someone who is not used to sailing might get _____, or seasick, on his or her first voyage. A sailor explores or travels the seas, but a[n] _____ travels through space.

4. List as many words as you can think of that contain the roots *multi* and *nov.*

Exercise IV

Inference

Complete the sentences by inferring information about the italicized word from its context.

1. A *narcissistic* person might refuse to help someone because...

2. If you have *qualms* about doing something, then you might...

3. People who cannot control their wants and pursue lives of *decadence* are in danger of...

Exercise V

Writing

Here is a writing prompt similar to the one you will find on the essay writing portion of the ACT.

> With the rise in the frequency of flash mobs, some cities have imposed early curfews upon minors. Curfews are not uncommon during times of catastrophe or martial law, but are they fair in normal times? Do curfews comply with the tenets of a free society, or do they tread close to tyranny? Do minors have legitimate reasons to be on the streets at night, or should they even need a reason?
>
> Take a position on the use of youth curfews and explain it in a letter to the editor of a city newspaper. Support your argument with three examples or subtopics detailing why curfews are appropriate or inappropriate means of maintaining order.

Thesis: Write a one-sentence response to the assignment. Make certain this single sentence offers a clear statement of your position.

Example: A curfew is one of the ultimate abuses of the rights of teenagers.

_____

_____

Organizational Plan: List at least three subtopics you will use to support your main idea. This list is your outline.

1. _____

2. _____

3. _____

Draft: Following your outline, write a good first draft of your essay. Remember to support all your points with examples, facts, references to reading, etc.

Review and Revise: Exchange essays with a classmate. Using the Holistic scoring guide on page 221, score your partner's essay (while he or she scores yours). If necessary, rewrite your essay to correct the problems noted by your partner.

Exercise VI

English Practice

Identifying Sentence Errors

Identify the errors in the following sentences. Choose the answer that fixes the error. If the sentence contains no error, select NO CHANGE.

1. My oldest <u>sister, Marilyn a</u> talented commercial artist, is also a registered nurse.
   A. NO CHANGE
   B. sister Marilyn a
   C. sister; Marilyn a
   D. sister, Marilyn, a

2. Arguing with a professor in class <u>will wreck havoc</u> with your grade.
   F. NO CHANGE
   G. will reek havoc
   H. will wreak havoc
   J. will reckon havoc

3. If the repaired car were ready to be driven, we <u>would of taken</u> it home.
   A. NO CHANGE
   B. would have taken
   C. would of took
   D. would have took

4. The nurse <u>suddenly jumps when</u> the doctor walked through the door to the operating room.
   F. NO CHANGE
   G. suddenly jumps after
   H. suddenly jumped when
   J. suddenly jumped while

5. I do not like <u>Shelly playing</u> of the radio so loudly in the car.
   A. NO CHANGE
   B. Shelly, to play
   C. Shelly; playing
   D. Shelly's playing

Improving Sentences

The underlined portion of each sentence below contains some flaw. Select the answer that best corrects the flaw.

6. I could watch the lake all day long playing computer solitaire is my only distraction.
    F. While I could watch the lake all day long and playing computer solitaire is my only distraction.
    G. All day long playing computer solitaire is my only distraction when I could be watching the lake.
    H. Playing computer solitaire all day long watching the lake is my only distraction.
    J. I could watch the lake all day long. Playing computer solitaire is my only distraction.

7. The diver, running out of air, tried to breath slow.
    A. breath slowly.
    B. breathe slow.
    C. breathe slowly.
    D. breath slower.

8. The dog was released by Stephanie and the guests were startled by the cheese platter when that was knocked on the floor by it.
    F. Stephanie released the dog and it startled the guests when the cheese platter was knocked onto the floor.
    G. When Stephanie released the dog, it knocked the guests onto the floor with the cheese platter.
    H. Stephanie released the dog, and it startled the guests when it knocked the cheese platter onto the floor.
    J. Stephanie released the dog and the guests were startled when it knocked the cheese platter onto the floor.

9. Some teenagers were suspended for failing grades this year on Monday.
    A. This year some teenagers were suspended for failing grades on Monday.
    B. On Monday, some teenagers were suspended for having failing grades this year.
    C. For failing grades Monday, some teenagers were suspended this year.
    D. Suspended for failing grades this year, some teenagers were suspended on Monday.

10. Henry bought a new computer that has a large memory and having a DVD burner.
    F. and a DVD burner.
    G. that has a DVD burner.
    H. for the DVD burner.
    J. with a DVD burner.

**Vocabulary
Power Plus
for the ACT**

Vocabulary,
Reading, and Writing
Exercises for High Scores

Lesson Ten

1. **fallible** (fal´ ə bəl) *adj.* capable of error
   All humans are *fallible* and sometimes make mistakes.
   syn: imperfect   ant: infallible; flawless

2. **blatant** (blāt´ nt) *adj.* obvious; too conspicuous
   His *blatant* efforts to get the girl's attention were embarrassing to everyone.
   syn: unconcealed; deliberate   *ant: secretive; cautious*

3. **dawdle** (dôd´ l) *v.* to waste time
   Bill, not wanting to go back to work, *dawdled* in the break room.
   syn: tarry; loiter   *ant: hasten; expedite*

4. **affiliate** (ə fil´ ē it) *n.* an associate; partner
   He denied that he was an *affiliate* of any organized-crime families.
   syn: member; colleague

5. **fawn** (fôn) *v.* to act slavishly submissive
   The young dancers *fawned* over the master of the ball and longed to be his partner.
   syn: grovel   *ant: ignore; disregard; neglect*

6. **calumny** (kal´ əm nē) *n.* a false and malicious accusation
   The candidate said that the accusation against him was just a *calumny* meant to damage his reputation.
   syn: slander; slur   *ant: compliment*

7. **berate** (bi rāt´) *v.* to scold or rebuke severely and at length
   The coach *berated* the three players for arriving at the game late.
   syn: admonish; reprimand   *ant: praise*

8. **minion** (min´ yən) *n.* a fawning, servile follower
   The bully's *minions* obeyed him not out of loyalty, but out of fear.
   syn: lackey   *ant: leader*

9. **desolate** (des´ ə lit) *adj.* lonely; forlorn; uninhabited; barren
   The castaway spent four years on a *desolate* island, many miles from the mainland.
   syn: deserted; bleak   *ant: populous; cheerful*

10. **bane** (bān) *n.* the cause of ruin, harm, distress, or death
The *bane* of the defeated alien invaders turned out to be the common cold.
syn: blight; curse   *ant: aid; assistance*

11. **pacify** (pas´ ə fī) *v.* to calm down
Grandmother was able to *pacify* the irritable baby.
syn: appease; placate   *ant: provoke; agitate*

12. **garble** (gär´ bəl) *v.* to mix up or distort
Jill's speech was good, except that she *garbled* some sentences.
syn: jumble; corrupt

13. **prevaricate** (pri vâr´ i kāt) *v.* to lie
When asked about the crime, Jim *prevaricated* because he did not want to
incriminate his friend.
syn: hedge

14. **filch** (filch) *v.* to steal
The woman *filched* my purse when I left the room to answer the telephone.
syn: pilfer; pinch

15. **neophyte** (nē´ ə fīt) *n.* a beginner
Though Sara was a *neophyte* at golf, she outplayed most of the veterans.
syn: novice; amateur   *ant: expert; veteran*

Exercise I

Words in Context

*From the list below, supply the words needed to complete the paragraph. Some
words will not be used.*

calumny	dawdle	minion	garble
bane	affiliate	prevaricate	

1. To avoid prosecution, the crime boss relied on his _____ to do his
dirty work for him. The _____ of the organization knew that if they
were arrested, they took the fall alone; however, the boss's overconfidence
in his associates caused his imprisonment when Knox, a killer, testified
against him in court. The boss claimed, of course, that the testimony was
merely a spiteful _____ designed to embarrass him; however, he
could not _____ cleverly enough to convince the jury that he was
innocent. Knox, now more a hero than _____ on society, went free.

From the list below, supply the words needed to complete the paragraph. Some words will not be used.

dawdle	minion	berate	blatant
filch	fawn	pacify	

2. Gina couldn't stand her friend's _____ attempt to get Lonnie to ask her to the dance. For weeks, Jamie _____ over Lonnie, even though he barely recognized her when they passed in the hall. Occasionally, Gina _____ her friend for being so foolish.

   "Don't _____ and wait for him," Gina would say. "The dance is tomorrow; ask someone you actually know." Jamie usually got angry when Gina lectured her.

   "Will you leave me alone, please?" Gina often replied. "I'm almost ready to take my dog to the dance just to _____ you!"

From the list below, supply the words needed to complete the paragraph. Some words will not be used.

neophyte	bane	fallible	filch
garble	desolate	prevaricate	

3. "Even the most experienced hikers are _____ in climates as harsh as this one," said the desert guide as he turned and squinted at the miles of _____ sand dunes that stretched to the horizon. "If there's one message that must not be _____, it's to bring plenty of water. You _____ who haven't hiked in the desert before will soon learn that once you're out there in the dunes, water is nonexistent. What you manage to _____ from the various plants or from beneath the ground will not be enough to sustain you."

Exercise II

Sentence Completion

Complete the sentence in a way that shows you understand the meaning of the italicized vocabulary word.

1. *Affiliates* of the organization were invited to…

2. Craig *garbles* his speech when…

3. I'm just a *neophyte* at this card game, so please…

4. In a small town, spreading *calumny* about someone could…

5. That sports car is bound to be your *bane* if you continue to…

6. The *desolate* barn was the perfect place for…

7. If you *dawdle* all night, you won't…

8. The cab driver *berated* the pedestrian who…

9. Nicole learned that even computers can be *fallible* when she…

10. Some of the fans at the concert *fawned* over…

11. The pickpocket must have *filched* my wallet when he…

12. When asked by his wife how she looked in the new dress, Randy *prevaricated* because he thought…

13. Neil was asked to leave the restaurant after his *blatant* attempt to…

14. The crooked government official was never arrested because it was his *minions* who…

15. Jennie had to *pacify* her dog after it…

Exercise III

Roots, Prefixes, and Suffixes

Study the entries and answer the questions that follow.

The roots *corp* and *corpor* mean "body."
The root *rupt* means "to break."
The prefix *inter* means "between" or "among."

1. *Using literal translations as guidance, define the following words without using a dictionary.*

   A. corporal   D. interrupt
   B. corporation   E. erupt
   C. incorporate   F. corrupt

2. If someone's appendix *ruptures*, then it _____. If a bank has no money, then it can be described as _____.

3. List as many words as you can think of that contain the roots *corp, rupt,* or the prefix *inter*.

Exercise IV

Inference

Complete the sentences by inferring information about the italicized word from its context.

1. If you *dawdle* too long before leaving for the airport, you might...

2. Since Ben's answering machine *garbled* the incoming message, Ben did not...

3. If police are trying to *pacify* the crowd, then people in the crowd must be...

Exercise V

Critical Reading

Below is a reading passage followed by several multiple-choice questions similar to the ones you will encounter on the ACT. Carefully read the passage and choose the best answer for each of the questions.

The following passage describes a couple who have not allowed sightlessness to impede their energetic lifestyle.

1   There is one style of golf that professionals have yet to experience. The style is to shut the eyes tightly, tee up, and then drive the little white ball toward the first hole. Who but a sightless person could imagine playing golf that way on every outing? Is there anything more unbelievable than trying to play golf without being able to see the club, the ball, the tee, and the course?

2   At least two golfers, Mary and Joe, always play golf that way. Mary and Joe were born blind; they have never had the luxury of seeing where their drives land—on the course or off.

3   The couple recently spent time with friends in the country, and after a few days of lawn parties, shopping trips, dining out, and neighborhood strolling, the foursome went golfing at a college course where Mary and Joe were reportedly the first blind people to golf.

4   According to Joe, golf is something different to do. It is a good form of outdoor recreation and exercise. He took up golf a few years ago when he began to have a little free time, and surprisingly, golf is fairly tame compared to the couple's other endeavors, such as canoeing and downhill skiing. Mary enjoys the summer outdoor activity as much as her winter bowling league, which she joined to alleviate the boredom that cold weather brings to outdoor types.

5   Joe says his long game of golf is better than his short; Mary, however, putts as close to the mark as most other golfers. Her ball frequently rolls to within one or two feet from the pin after thirty-foot putts on the green.

6   Learning to play golf is not much different for the blind than for the sighted, says Joe, and the clubs are exactly the same. Coaches who accompany Mary and Joe on golf outings have had their techniques handed down from past trainers of the blind, and the only extra guidance the players get is a verbal point in the right direction before they hit. Rules and regulations remain the same as for sighted golfers; there are no gimmies just because a player literally can't see the lie before the shot. For practice, Mary and Joe go to driving and putting ranges. There, a coach sets up the shots and positions the golfers so that they hit the ball when they swing. The golfers then work on perfecting their swings and directing their shots. They strive for consistency and good contact with the ball, listening for that great sound that every golfer longs to hear when the club smacks the ball just right. Mary and Joe are in their second year on the links, and they have graduated from playing nine-hole games to playing eighteen-hole games.

7   Navigation on a golf course, in a bowling alley, or behind a boat pulling them on water skis (where they say they can hear the wake on each side of them), is no

big deal for this athletic pair; in fact, they are at a point at which their own guide dogs cannot always accompany them on their adventures. When Mary and Joe hit the slopes, the guide dogs must stay home because of the potential danger to other skiers. Dogs are not welcome on golf courses or tennis courts, either.

8   While Mary and Joe love sports, they also have, between the two of them, over forty years of high-level office experience. With assistance from the guide dogs, Mary and Joe use foot power and public transportation to navigate from the suburbs to their offices in the bustling city.

9   The couple have many other outside interests, including membership in advocacy organizations, sports leagues, religious affiliations, and volunteer networks. They are not unaware of the many so-called comical remarks of sighted people about those without vision, but they often lead the conversation by making fun of themselves. Mary and Joe are down-to-earth people who have never asked any favors because of their blindness, and they do not expect to be treated any differently from anyone else.

10   In the unique setting of a golf course, it is unusual to watch a blind couple enjoying such a precise sport. It is more unusual to consider that in the short time that they have been playing, Mary and Joe have better golf games than many of their sighted friends have. One can only imagine how their friends feel.

1. According to the passage, how did Mary and Joe lose their sight?
    A. Joe was born blind, and Mary went blind in childhood.
    B. When they were both ten, a disease took their sight.
    C. They were both born blind.
    D. Mary is partially sighted, and Joe went blind during college.

2. According to paragraph 4, Joe took up golf when
    F. he had free time.
    G. he needed exercise.
    H. he wanted outdoor recreation.
    J. he wanted to compete with Mary

3. According to paragraph 6, the main difference between golf for sighted people and golf for blind people is
    A. the length of the clubs.
    B. the size of the putting clubs.
    C. the use of verbal directions.
    D. the rules and regulations.

4. As used in paragraph 6, *lie* most nearly means
    F. an untruth.
    G. the flight of the ball.
    H. the guide dog.
    J. the position of the ball.

5. During practice, which of the following indicates to Mary and Joe that they are hitting well?
   A. the sound of a well-hit ball
   B. eighteen-hole golf courses
   C. the feel of the swing
   D. the number of years that they have been playing

6. How do Mary and Joe manage to get to their places of employment?
   F. by taxi and scooter
   G. by public transportation and walking
   H. by hitchhiking and train
   J. by guide dog and taxi

7. How do Mary and Joe handle jokes about blindness?
   A. They reprimand the joke tellers.
   B. They secretly scorn the joke tellers.
   C. They walk away angry.
   D. They make fun of themselves.

8. Which could you infer from the following sentences?

   > It is more unusual to consider that in the short time that they have been playing, Mary and Joe have better golf games than many of their sighted friends. One can only imagine how their friends feel.

   F. Friends might be chagrined if they lose at golf to Mary and Joe.
   G. Friends take advantage of Mary and Joe.
   H. Mary and Joe have blind friends.
   J. The friends like to golf with Mary and Joe.

9. Which of the following statements best identifies the point of the article?
   A. Golf is a good game.
   B. Optimism is a type of game.
   C. Anything is possible with diligent effort.
   D. Playing golf is possible for sightless people.

10. Of the following types of publications, which would be most likely to publish this article?
    F. country home and garden magazine
    G. instruction brochure
    H. local newspaper column
    J. book about golf techniques

Level Nine

Vocabulary
Power Plus
for the
ACT
Vocabulary,
Reading, and Writing
Exercises for High Scores

Lesson Eleven

1. **flagrant** (flā´ grənt) *adj.* glaringly bad; outrageous
   His *flagrant* disregard for authority caused the boy a lot of trouble.
   syn: offensive; shameless; brazen

2. **patrician** (pə trish´ ən) *n.* an aristocrat
   The *patrician* could not marry the man she loved, because he was a member
   of the working class.
   syn: noble   *ant: commoner*

3. **emissary** (em´ i ser ē) *n.* one sent on a special mission to represent others
   Prior to the concept of diplomatic immunity, an *emissary* was often
   imprisoned or killed.
   syn: ambassador; agent

4. **kindred** (kin´ drid) *adj.* having similar origin, nature, or character
   They had met only days ago, but the two girls were *kindred* spirits and
   immediately became friends.
   syn: homogeneous   *ant: disparate*

5. **fracas** (frā´ kəs) *n.* a loud quarrel or fight
   The coaches broke up the *fracas* that had begun on the playing field during
   the game.
   syn: brawl

6. **lacerate** (las´ ə rāt) *v.* to tear (flesh) jaggedly
   The pedal *lacerated* the rider's leg when the bicycle flipped over.
   syn: slash; gash; rip   *ant: suture*

7. **futile** (fyo̅o̅t´ l) *adj.* useless; pointless
   I received a shock during my *futile* attempt to fix the television set.
   syn: ineffectual; fruitless   *ant: effective; useful*

8. **immaculate** (im mak´ yə lit) *adj.* spotless; perfect
   The rooms of the mansion were as *immaculate* as the grounds surrounding
   the large estate.
   syn: clean; pureant: dirty; soiled; spotted

9. **gait** (gāt) *n.* manner of walking
   The horse's smooth *gait* made riding easy.
   syn: walk

10. **carp** (kärp) *v.* to complain or to find fault in a petty or nagging way
No one wants to talk to you because you *carp* about every little thing.
syn: grumble; nag; nitpick   *ant: praise; laud*

11. **query** (kwēr´ ē) *v.* to ask; inquire
The buyer decided to *query* the previous owners about the leaky plumbing
before buying the house.
syn: question; interrogate

12. **queue** (kyōō) *n.* a line of people or vehicles
During the war, *queues* formed in front of butcher shops because meat was
in short supply.

13. **nefarious** (nə fâr´ ē əs) *adj.* very wicked; notorious
Billy the Kid was one of the most *nefarious* characters of the Old West.
syn: villainous; despicable   *ant: reputable; honest*

14. **genesis** (jen´ ə sis) *n.* beginning; origin
The invention of the telegraph marked the *genesis* of the Information Age.
syn: start; birth ant: conclusion; finish

15. **facade** (fə säd´) *n.* a deceptive outward appearance; a misrepresentation
Joan's cheerful *facade* did not hide her depression.
syn: pretense; charade

Exercise I

Words in Context

From the list below, supply the words needed to complete the paragraph. Some words will not be used.

gait	futile	kindred	immaculate
emissary	query	nefarious	facade

1. When Cal took a job working at the docks, he didn't realize that he was
    going to become a[n] _____ for a[n] _____ businessman who
    made a fortune shipping black-market goods. After one week of unloading
    crates from ships and putting them on trucks during the graveyard shift,
    Cal _____ the supervisor as to the contents of the heavy wood boxes.
    The question was _____; the supervisor just looked at Cal, paused for
    an uneasy moment, and then replied, "Tractor parts." At that moment, Cal
    realized that he was participating in a[n] _____ that concealed some
    type of illegal operation; even worse, he was a pawn for the businessman—
    if U.S. Customs were to raid the dock, Cal would probably be arrested while
    the boss's record remained _____.

From the list below, supply the words needed to complete the paragraph. Some words will not be used.

genesis	emissary	gait
queue	patrician	carp

2. After six hours of driving, Charlie parked his car and walked across the
    parking lot with an odd _____. He was happy to stretch his legs, but
    he _____ about summer crowds when he saw that the _____
    for the restroom extended around the corner of the rest stop. He should
    have expected as much, he reasoned: Memorial Day weekend was the
    _____ of every summer season. With the summer season, of course,
    come summer crowds.

From the list below, supply the words needed to complete the paragraph. Some words will not be used.

flagrant	immaculate	lacerate	fracas
patrician	kindred	nefarious	

3. Most of the servants abandoned the grounds when they heard the
_____ outside the front gates. A crowd of armed peasants gathered
below, preparing to punish their _____ for what they described
as a[n] _____ abuse of his title. Disease and famine were rampant
throughout the villages of the manor, but Lord Geoffrey continued to raise
taxes and host feasts for the nearby aristocrats, all of whom shared many
_____ beliefs about the peasants. Nervously, Geoffrey peered from
his chamber window to see his guards surrendering to the mob. The angry
farmers and merchants did not _____ the guards with their pitchforks
and poorly fashioned swords, but Geoffrey knew that they would not be so
merciful with him. In a fit of panic, he began thinking of possible escape
routes as the mob flooded into the courtyard through the gate.

Exercise II

Sentence Completion

Complete the sentence in a way that shows you understand the meaning of the italicized vocabulary word.

1. A *fracas* developed in the parking lot after…

2. Every day during work, the customer service representative had to listen to people *carp* about…

3. In American culture, it is a *flagrant* act of disrespect to…

4. The largely outnumbered army built hundreds of fires at night to create a *facade* that…

5. The *queue* at the ticket window was so long that Kim decided to…

6. The broken glass on the floor will *lacerate* your feet if you do not…

7. You should *query* the post office about the package if…

8. The officer suspected that something *nefarious* was occurring in the bank when he saw…

9. The photograph in the guide showed an *immaculate* park area, but the real park was…

10. Before the *genesis* of the age of automobiles, people relied on…

11. The affluent *patrician* knew that his family would frown upon him for…

12. Despite their *kindred* roots, the two brothers…

13. Serena knew that if she didn't approach the podium with a confident *gait*, the audience would…

14. The United Nations sent an *emissary* to the poverty-stricken nation to…

15. Efforts to contain the floodwaters proved *futile* when…

Exercise III

Roots, Prefixes, and Suffixes

Study the entries and answer the questions that follow.

The root *am* means "friend" or "to love."
The root *aqu* means "water."
The root *brev* means "short."
The root *prot* means "first" or "original."

1. Using literal translations as guidance, define the following words without using a dictionary.

    A. amicable   D. aquatic
    B. amative   E. prototype
    C. aquarium   F. protagonist

2. If a word is long and you don't want to write it out, you might simply use its _____. If a speaker is known for her *brevity*, then her speeches must be _____.

3. Someone in a loving mood might be described as being _____. That person might be in love with, or _____ of, someone else.

4. List as many words as you can think of that contain the roots *aqu* or *prot*.

Exercise IV

Inference

Complete the sentences by inferring information about the italicized word from its context.

1. If you *carp* about the decorations in your friend's new home, then your friend might not...

2. A criminal who is imprisoned for *nefarious* crimes must have done things that...

3. If a particular approach to solving a problem seems *futile*, then you should...

Exercise V

Writing

Here is a writing prompt similar to the one you will find on the essay writing portion of the ACT.

Math, language, and science will always be the core of education, but that core curriculum accounts for only a small proportion of the classes you take in high school. At one time in America, the core curriculum included certain practical courses such as wood and metal shop, home economics, and typing, among others.

If you could add three courses to the core curriculum, what would they be, and why? Consider the skills that you think would be valuable to you one day, whether during your education, or twenty years from now. Your suggestions might even include activities you enjoy, or skills that require more practical experience than is found in traditional textbooks and quizzes.

Your essay should be in the form of a letter to the Department of Education. Be sure to explain why each of your three choices would be valuable and legitimate additions to the curriculum. Your suggestions might be interesting to you, but you have to sell your ideas to a school board.

Thesis: Write a one-sentence response to the assignment. Make certain this single sentence offers a clear statement of your position.

Example: Courses that allow students to be self-reliant are especially important, and the first to add to a curriculum should be a course on basic auto repair.

_____

_____

Organizational Plan: List at least three subtopics you will use to support your main idea. This list is your outline.

1. _____

2. _____

3. _____

Draft: Following your outline, write a good first draft of your essay. Remember to support all your points with examples, facts, references to reading, etc.

Review and Revise: Exchange essays with a classmate. Using the scoring guide for Organization on page 216, score your partner's essay (while he or she scores yours). Focus on the organizational plan and use of language conventions. If necessary, rewrite your essay to improve the organizational plan and/or your use of language.

Exercise VI

English Practice

Improving Paragraphs

Read the following passage and then choose the best revision for the underlined portions of the paragraph. The questions will require you to make decisions regarding the revision of the reading selection. Some revisions are not of actual mistakes, but will improve the clarity of the writing.

[1]

(1) While riding on a roller coaster moving seventy miles per hour, you probably need to squint your eyes to see, or they well up with tears. (2) Your hair and your shirt flap in the wind like streamers, and your hat, if you wore one, have long departed.

1. Which of the following
   suggestions corrects the error
   in sentence 2?
   A. Replace *you* with *one*
      would.
   B. Replace *have* with *has.*
   C. Replace *flap* with *flaps.*
   D. Combine both sentences.

[2]

(3) Now imagine that you are in freefall, 5,000 feet above the surface of the earth, and you have just reached a terminal velocity of 120 miles per hour. (4) Seeing anything without goggles is impossible, and the material of your jumpsuit flaps so quickly that it makes a buzzing sound. (5) Now picture yourself in the cockpit of a fighter jet <u>thats</u>² plummeting toward earth at 800 miles per hour, faster than sound, and faster than some bullets. (6) You're at 10,000 feet, and the aircraft is out of control. (7) If you stay with the plane, you will die in seconds. (8) If you eject, you might be killed instantly. (9) Is it <u>unimaginable.</u>³ (10) Not for Captain Brian Udell.

2. F. NO CHANGE
   G. that's
   H. that's,
   J. that was

3. A. NO CHANGE
   B. unimaginable?
   C. unimaginable:
   D. unimaginable!

4. Which of the following changes to paragraph 2 would improve the flow of the passage?
   F. Change *unimaginable* to *unthinkable.*
   G. Combine sentences 3 and 4.
   H. Insert a comma after *flaps.*
   J. Begin a new paragraph after sentence 4.

[3]

(11) During a nighttime Air Force training sortie off the coast of North Carolina, the instruments in Captain Udell's F-15E Strike Eagle malfunctioned. (12) Some <u>censors</u>⁵ told him everything was fine, while others suggested a pending disaster. (13) The heads-up display indicated that his flight status was normal, but, according to other (functioning) indicators, his jet was plummeting straight to earth at nearly supersonic speed. (14) In little more than a second, Udell <u>gave, Dennis White,</u>⁶ the weapons system officer, the order to bail out, and by the time the canopy blew at 5,000 feet, the jet had accelerated to over 780 miles per hour—1,200 feet per second.

5. A. NO CHANGE
   B. censers
   C. scenters
   D. sensors

6. F. NO CHANGE
   G. gave; Dennis White,
   H. gave Dennis White,
   J. gave, to Dennis White,

7. Which unnecessary sentence should be deleted from paragraph 3?
   A. Sentence 11
   B. Sentence 12
   C. Sentence 13
   D. Sentence 14

[4]

(15) Udell's ACES II ejection seat cleared the aircraft at 3,000 feet above the ocean. (16) Air resistance at Mach 1 shredded Udell as he slowed to subsonic speeds; but luckily, his <u>shoot functioned</u>[8] and caught the air at less than 1,000 feet, had he hesitated just one half-second longer, the chute would not have deployed in time, and the impact on the water would have killed him.

8. F. NO CHANGE
   G. shute functioned
   H. chute functioned
   J. shoot functions

9. Which suggestion would correct a grammatical error in paragraph 4?
   A. Put a period after *1000 feet* and capitalize *had*.
   B. Change *ACES* to lowercase letters.
   C. Replace *killed* with *hurt*.
   D. Combine sentences 15 and 16.

[5]

(17) Don't ask Udell what is was like to travel at Mach 1 without the luxury of a plane; he is glad to have no memory of the three seconds that followed the pull of the ejection lever. (18) He <u>recollects his descent only</u>[10] to the water, pulling his broken body into a waterlogged raft and then discovering how the ejection had battered his body. (19) His mask and helmet <u>has been</u>[11] stripped from his head, and anything he had in his pockets had torn through. (20) His flight suit was shredded, and the skin of his face was stretched and swollen. (21) His arm and ankle <u>was</u>[12] dislocated, his rib was cracked, and the tendons in his right knee were so damaged that his lower leg flopped uselessly onto his other leg when he flipped it into the raft. (22) The injuries were substantial, but the price was relatively <u>small. Captain</u>[13] White, the weapons officer, did not survive the ejection. (23) Udell waited alone, cold and broken in the dark water, for four hours before the Coast Guard located him. (24) Two months and several surgeries after the unfortunate night, Brian Udell walked again. (25) Eight months later, Udell was back in the cockpit, but the lifelong pilot (he learned to fly when he was nine), had a different perspective of his aviation career: it would always be second to the family he almost left behind.

10. F. NO CHANGE
    G. recollects his only descent
    H. only recollects his descent
    J. recollects only his descent

11. A. NO CHANGE
    B. had been
    C. have been
    D. was

12. F. NO CHANGE
    G. were
    H. where
    J. we're

13. A. NO CHANGE
    B. small Captain
    C. small. Captain
    D. small: Captain

14. Revising the first two paragraphs from second person (you) to third person perspective would probably:
    F. create a more scholarly tone for the passage.
    G. diminish the author's intended effect upon the reader.
    H. cause the beginning of the passage to conflict with the remaining portion.
    J. make the passage seem too opinionated.

15. What would best conclude the passage?
    A. End with a quotation from Udell's wife.
    B. In one more paragraph, compare Udell's experience to an automobile race.
    C. Include a paragraph about Udell's family.
    D. Begin a new paragraph after *Coast Guard located him.*

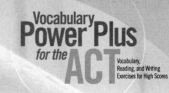

Vocabulary
Power Plus
for the **ACT**
Vocabulary,
Reading, and Writing
Exercises for High Scores

Lesson Twelve

1. **deluge** (del´ yōōj) *n.* a flood; an overwhelming rush
   The new amusement park experienced a *deluge* of visitors on opening day.
   syn: inundation; surge   *ant: drought; dearth*

2. **catholic** (kath´ ə lik) *adj.* universal; wide-ranging
   His *catholic* interests made him quite knowledgeable in many subjects.
   syn: broad   *ant: provincial; limited; parochial*

3. **eerie** (ēr´ ē) *adj.* weird; mysterious; strange and frightening
   No one accepted the dare to stay in the *eerie* old mansion for one night.
   syn: creepy; sinister   *ant: common; ordinary*

4. **martial** (mär´ shəl) *adj.* warlike; relating to the military
   A state of *martial* law was declared in the small country in the weeks
   following the overthrow of the government.

5. **anthropomorphic** (an´ thrə pə môr´ fik) *adj.* attributing human
      characteristics or qualities to objects, animals, or concepts
   Anthropomorphic stories might feature pigs and rabbits walking upright,
   wearing clothes, and speaking to each other in human languages.

6. **beneficiary** (ben ə fish´ ē er ē) *n.* one who receives benefits
   John was the sole *beneficiary* of his Uncle Martin's vast estate.
   syn: recipient; heir

7. **careen** (kə rēn´) *v.* to swerve or lurch from side to side while in motion
   The torrential winds caused the ship to *careen* violently.
   syn: tilt

8. **aplomb** (ə plum´) *n.* self-confidence
   The *aplomb* of the young dancer astonished the veterans of the troupe.
   syn: assurance; poise   *ant: awkwardness*

9. **guile** (gīl) *n.* slyness and cunning in dealing with others
   Brad's *guile* contributed to his wealth, but it also created enemies.
   syn: craftiness; astuteness   *ant: honesty*

10. **modicum** (mod´ i kəm) *n.* a small amount
A sudden shower gave us a *modicum* of relief from the heat and humidity.
syn: bit   *ant: abundance*

11. **fester** (fes´ tər) *v.* to grow embittered over time; to rot
If allowed to *fester*, dislike can turn into bitter hatred.
syn: aggravate; worsen

12. **languish** (lang´ gwish) *v.* to become weak or feeble; to lose strength
I *languished* in bed all day, hoping to avoid all the work that still needed to be done.
syn: wither; fade   *ant: thrive*

13. **pall** (pôl) *n.* something that covers or conceals
A *pall* of gloom descended over the crowd.
syn: shroud

14. **havoc** (hav´ ək) *n.* great destruction; chaos
The commandos wreaked *havoc* throughout the area when they infiltrated the secret base.
syn: mayhem; disorder   *ant: order*

15. **rancid** (ran´ sid) *adj.* having a bad taste or smell; spoiled
The bitter fight over child custody left a *rancid* taste in both lawyers' mouths.
syn: rotten; repulsive   *ant: fresh*

Exercise I

Words in Context

From the list below, supply the words needed to complete the paragraph. Some words will not be used.

deluge	**pall**	**careen**	**fester**
modicum	**martial**	**beneficiary**	

1. Everyone anticipated the opening of the new state park, but not the strict, almost _____ rules and prohibitions that imposed fines for camping, cooking, swimming, or walking in unauthorized areas. Immediately after the park opened, the Department of Parks and Recreation received a[n] _____ of letters questioning who, exactly, the _____ of the new park were supposed to be, since the people who paid for the park apparently were not. Without at least a[n] _____ of freedom to explore the old forest, people complained, the park was simply private property. Most agreed that the park would be wonderful without the _____ of restrictions hanging over it.

From the list below, supply the words needed to complete the paragraph. Some words will not be used.

fester	**aplomb**	**guile**	**havoc**
languish	**rancid**	**pall**	

2. The power outage brought _____ to the meat processing plant. For hours, workers _____ in the dark before struggling to move tons of perishable food to refrigerated trailers to prevent it from _____ in the rapidly warming warehouse. Any meat left in the facility after a designated time was declared _____ and marked for disposal. Many workers worried about the fate of the company, but the owner reassured them and asked them, with great _____, to keep their composure through the crisis.

From the list below, supply the words needed to complete the paragraph. Some words will not be used.

catholic	eerie	**martial**	careen
guile	rancid	**anthropomorphic**	

3. The children's book features _____ animal characters that speak and interact as though they were people. In the story, a sneaky wolf uses his _____ to manipulate a chicken into leaving its pen and entering the _____ old forest behind the farm. The wolf, of course, then tries to eat the chicken, but it _____ around rocks and trees, causing the wolf to become dizzy and give up the chase. Like many children's books, this one has _____ themes that appeal to all audiences.

Exercise II

Sentence Completion

Complete the sentence in a way that shows you understand the meaning of the italicized vocabulary word.

1. The youth camp is designed to build up the *aplomb* of children by...

2. Eric expected to find *eerie* paintings hanging on the walls when he...

3. The cat *languished* in...

4. She knew that the milk was *rancid* because...

5. The producers wanted the new sitcom to be *catholic* enough to appeal to...

6. Renee has the *guile* to become...

7. Sandy thought the rules in her new school seemed almost *martial* because...

9. Randy wanted only a *modicum* of silence after a long day of...

10. A *deluge* of customers swamped the store on the day that...

11. Tim was Howard's *beneficiary*, so when Howard died, Tim...

12. The potato salad will *fester* in the sun, so you should...

13. Foods that wreak *havoc* on your teeth include...

14. The smog created a *pall* that...

15. The car *careened* all over the highway when the driver...

Exercise III

Roots, Prefixes, and Suffixes

Study the entries and answer the questions that follow.

The roots *patr* and *patern* mean "father."
The root *scop* means "to watch."
The roots *scrib* and *script* mean "to write."
The root *cent* means "one hundred."

1. *Using literal translations as guidance, define the following words without using a dictionary.*

   A. manuscript D. centennial
   B. scripture E. percent
   C. scribe F. horoscope

2. To see things far away, you might watch them through a[n] _____, but to see tiny things, might use a[n] _____.

3. *Arch* means "ruler," so a male leader of a family is called a[n] _____. If you talk down to someone as though you were the father and he were the child, you are said to _____ that person. A _____ test can verify that someone is the father of a child.

4. List as many words as you can think of that contain the roots *scrib* or *script*.

Exercise IV

Inference

Complete the sentences by inferring information about the italicized word from its context.

1. You are the *beneficiary* on my insurance policy, so if anything happens to me, you will…

2. *Anthropomorphic* animals in literature might speak English, drive cars, or do anything that makes them…

3. Only a *modicum* of readers claimed to dislike the…

Exercise V

Critical Reading

Below is a reading passage followed by several multiple-choice questions similar to the ones you will encounter on the ACT. Carefully read the passage and choose the best answer for each of the questions.

The following passage discusses famous suffragettes and the barriers that the suffragettes had to overcome.

Women have been fighting for equal rights since the middle of the nineteenth century. While some women argue that they still do not have equal rights, they cannot argue that the cause has come a long way since Elizabeth Cady Stanton and Susan B. Anthony took the first steps toward gaining the acceptance of women's suffrage.

5   Elizabeth Cady Stanton was a pioneer for women's rights before her time. At her own wedding, she appalled her guests by intentionally omitting the word "obey" while reciting her vows; fortunately, her husband supported her views that women were equal to men. Driven by her cause, Stanton—a mother of seven children—

10 made time to become a leading activist for the rights of women. She wrote speeches for Susan B. Anthony, she spoke at numerous women's rights conventions, and, using the Declaration of Independence for inspiration, she drafted the 1848 Seneca Falls declaration. New Englanders were familiar with the powerful rhetoric in her

15 speeches. She believed that women were morally superior and therefore deserved the right to participate in politics.

    Susan B. Anthony, born in Massachusetts, was also a pioneer in the women's rights arena. While a young schoolgirl, Anthony questioned her teacher as to why

20 he taught long division only to boys. He explained that women did not need to know how to do long division—only how to read a Bible and run a home. Anthony then took it upon herself to learn long division by listening in on the teacher's long division lessons to the boys. Anthony became so prominent as a women's rights

25 advocate that women who joined the cause were called "Susie B's." One of Anthony's defining moments came when she, along with a few other women, registered to vote during the election of 1871. Fifteen women actually succeeded in voting, and though they were later arrested and fined, they did not fail in making history.

30   For every Stanton and Anthony who quested for rights, there were many men resisting their efforts, citing moral questions and physical limitations of women, as well as a host of other reasons that would be laughable to present sensibilities. The anti-suffragist platform included claims that women would be so exhausted

after walking to the poll that they would be too disoriented to vote wisely, and that
35 women wearing long-sleeved dresses would be able to cheat by concealing extra
ballots! One anti-suffrage warning, however, was more serious and not implausible:
that suffrage was a harbinger of destruction of the traditional family, because it
would blur the traditional gender roles of men and women and cause families to
40 fall apart. Women would assume the roles of men and lose their feminine qualities,
it was argued, and men, in turn, would become effeminate. In the decades since,
society has come to realize that a changing family structure, as opposed to the
intentional hobbling of women's intellects and participation in society, is not a
45 negative consequence of suffrage, but the product of an advancing civilization.

If it were not for the forerunners who took the first arduous steps toward
equality, women's rights would be nowhere near where they are today. These
difficult strides have secured a nation in which women are free to earn a living,
50 govern states, or run for president. Elizabeth Cady Stanton and Susan B. Anthony
deserve the thanks for over a century of progress, and many women look to them
as role models and inspiration.

1. The purpose of the passage is to
    A. inform.
    B. persuade.
    C. entertain.
    D. laud.

2. Which of the following is *not* a way that Stanton, as a leading activist,
   helped the cause of women's suffrage?
    F. leaving out "obey" from wedding vows
    G. writing speeches for Anthony
    H. drafting the Seneca Falls declaration
    J. speaking at women's rights conventions

3. As used in line 14, *rhetoric* most nearly means
    A. speaking.
    B. style of speaking.
    C. the study of principles and rules of composition.
    D. knowledge.

4. Which of the following is evidence of Anthony's widespread influence?
    F. She taught herself long division.
    G. Women who followed her were called "Susie B's."
    H. She registered to vote.
    J. She was able to cast a ballot.

5. In line 33, *platform* means
    A. theater stage.
    B. declaration of principles.
    C. point of view.
    D. place to speak.

6. According to the anti-suffragists, which was *not* a potential effect on family life if women were granted suffrage?
    F. Women would assume male responsibilities.
    G. Masculinity would become obsolete.
    H. Men would become effeminate.
    J. The family structure would fall apart.

7. As used in line 37, *harbinger* most nearly means
    A. an attack.
    B. an omen.
    C. a result.
    D. a deletion.

8. Which of the following is a product of an advancing civilization, according to the passage?
    F. Traditional family roles change.
    G. Women grow emotionally stable.
    H. People vote electronically.
    J. Men cease voting.

9   According to lines 41-45, preventing suffrage for women is akin to
    A. making men become nurses.
    B. putting women on a pedestal.
    C. keeping women uneducated.
    D. allowing women to run for office.

10. This passage would be best suited for
    F. a biography on Susan B. Anthony.
    G. a news blog.
    H. a general social studies book.
    J. a book on the history of the family.

Level Nine

Vocabulary
Power Plus
for the **ACT**
Vocabulary,
Reading, and Writing
Exercises for High Scores

Lesson Thirteen

1. **holocaust** (hol´ ə kôst) *n.* a great or complete destruction of life
    Many feared that the Cuban Missile Crisis was going to end in a nuclear
    holocaust.

2. **embroil** (em broil´) *v.* to draw into a conflict or fight
    The new zoning ordinance *embroiled* members of the planning committee.
    syn: entangle

3. **anachronism** (a nak´ rə niz əm) *n.* something or someone existing
      outside of its proper time
    Some consider the use of fossil fuels to be an *anachronism* in this age of
    nuclear technology.

4. **denigrate** (den´ i grāt) *v.* to attack the reputation of; to speak ill of
    The senator, who opposed political mudslinging, refused to *denigrate* his
    opponent.
    syn: defame; belittle   *ant: praise; promote*

5. **humane** (hyōō mān´) *adj.* kind; compassionate
    Putting the critically injured horse out of its misery is the most *humane*
    course of action.
    syn: kindly; benevolent; considerate   *ant: inhumane; cruel*

6. **effusive** (i fyōō´ siv) *adj.* emotionally excessive; overly demonstrative
    I don't argue with you in public because your *effusive* responses
    embarrass me.
    syn: gushing   *ant: reserved; restrained*

7. **defunct** (di fungkt´) *adj.* no longer in existence
    Don't get scammed into buying stock in a *defunct* corporation.
    syn: invalid; extinct

8. **lackey** (lak´ ē) *n.* a slavish follower
    I want to speak to the boss, not a *lackey* who screens visitors for him.
    syn: minion

9. **envisage** (en viz´ ij) *v.* to form a mental picture
    You should *envisage* the task before you begin it.
    syn: imagine; visualize

10. **lament** (lə ment´) *v.* to mourn
Devoted fans *lamented* the death of the popular singer.
syn: grieve   *ant: rejoice*

11. **gape** (gāp) *v.* to stare with an open mouth
The child *gaped* at his mother in astonishment when she switched off the television.

12. **impertinent** (im pûr´ tn ənt) *adj.* rude and disrespectful
The boy earned an after-school detention for his *impertinent* behavior.
syn: insolent; impolite   *ant: polite; courteous*

13. **haughty** (hô´ tē) *adj.* arrogant; proud
The poorly dressed visitor drew a *haughty* look from the butler.
syn: arrogant   *ant: humble; shy*

14. **nemesis** (nem´ i sis) *n.* someone or something a person cannot conquer or achieve; a hated enemy
Sherlock Holmes tried to outwit his *nemesis*, professor Moriarty.
syn: rival; adversary   *ant: collaborator; friend*

15. **lethal** (lē´ thəl) *adj.* deadly; fatal
The clean-up crew wore respirators to protect themselves from the *lethal* vapors.
syn: mortal   *ant: harmless*

Exercise I

Words in Context

From the list below, supply the words needed to complete the paragraph. Some words will not be used.

anachronism	lethal	effusive	gape
holocaust	defunct	embroil	

1. The argument over the reality of global warming _____ many scientists, most of whom disagreed. Some claimed that global warming will cause a planetary _____ in which nothing will survive. Other scientists were _____ in their arguments that claimed such _____ theories are meant only to cause worldwide panic. Indeed, they agree that global warming exists, but that it might take thousands of years to cause the climate to become _____. In a thousand years, or even a hundred years, they assert, the processes that cause global warming will be _____, replaced by new technologies.

From the list below, supply the words needed to complete the paragraph. Some words will not be used.

lackey	denigrate	lament	humane
anachronism	nemesis	defunct	

2. The elderly Carl knew that he was a[n] _____ among the young programmers working in his office. Each time he struggled to send a simple e-mail message, he _____ the death of the typewriter-and-telephone era in which he had spent most of his career. Bitter that the end of his own usefulness approached, Carl often _____ the young programmers for having no concept of how to use their own brains—not calculators—to solve equations or analyze data. Technology had become Carl's _____, he felt, and had turned him into a dinosaur. Sometimes, the young manager and his _____ mused at Carl's outdated experience with punch cards and mainframes, and it fueled Carl's resentment. He couldn't wait to retire.

From the list below, supply the words needed to complete the paragraph. Some words will not be used.

gape	envisage	humane	holocaust
impertinent	haughty	lackey	

3. "You know that it's _____ to stare and make faces," said the nanny in a[n] _____ tone. "_____ yourself in the same situation. How would you feel if every child who passed _____ at you as though you were a sideshow attraction? Learn to be a little more _____ toward your fellow man."

Exercise II

Sentence Completion

Complete the sentence in a way that shows you understand the meaning of the italicized vocabulary word.

1. George *denigrated* Suzanne by spreading rumors that she...

2. Pat *gaped* when she saw...

3. The character's cell phone was an *anachronism* in the movie because...

4. The famous actor traveled with a group of *lackeys* who...

5. The *haughty* salesman in the upscale jewelry shop told us that...

6. Since my car's manufacturer is now *defunct*, I cannot get...

7. During dinner, it's *impertinent* for you to...

8. The representative at the travel agency said, "*Envisage* yourself...

9. Greg became Aaron's *nemesis* when Greg...

10. The entire community *lamented* the...

11. When the *effusive* man found a bogus charge on his telephone bill, he...

12. The huge hurricane was a natural *holocaust* that...

13. It is not *humane* to leave your...

14. The devious businessman spread rumors that *embroiled* his...

15. The doctor reassured the patient that the substance she encountered was not *lethal* and that she would...

Exercise III

Roots, Prefixes, and Suffixes

Study the entries and answer the questions that follow.

The roots *pot* and *poss* mean "to be able."
The prefix *psych* means "mind."
The root *arm* means "tools" or "arms" (weapons).

1. Using literal translations as guidance, define the following words without using a dictionary.

    A. potential   D. psychology
    B. potent   E. alarm
    C. psyche   F. disarm

2. If no one can make the journey, it is said to be _____. An *impotent* worker is _____ to do a good job.

3. List as many words as you can think of that contain the roots *poss, pot,* and *arm.*

Exercise IV

Inference

Complete the sentences by inferring information about the italicized word from its context.

1. The teacher prefers to *denigrate* her students rather than...

2. If high tariffs on all goods *embroil* the colonists with the mother country, the colonists might...

3. Since the cave contained *lethal* amounts of poison gas, the rescuers had to...

> ### Exercise V
> # *Writing*

Here is a writing prompt similar to the one you will find on the essay writing portion of the ACT.

As society becomes more averse to violence, and politicians seize upon sensationalized events to use as justification to propose bills that often become laws, some schools have enacted bans on any form of physical contact between students. Some bans disallow far more from the already governed public displays of affection or fighting in the halls; the latest restrict everything. A simple tap on the shoulder or a hug to console a friend is now an offense that can blemish a permanent record.

Have schools forgotten the reality of day-to-day human existence? Are they enforcing impossible rules and forgoing discipline in the name of protecting students? Take a side in the argument for or against no-touching policies in schools and write a letter to your school board. Support your position with at least three subtopics based on your own observations and experience.

Thesis: Write a one-sentence response to the assignment. Make certain this single sentence offers a clear statement of your position.

Example: Students who lack enough discipline to keep their hands to themselves have no business graduating high school.

_____

_____

Organizational Plan: List at least three subtopics you will use to support your main idea. This list is your outline.

1. _____

2. _____

3. _____

Draft: Following your outline, write a good first draft of your essay. Remember to support all your points with examples, facts, references to reading, etc.

Review and Revise: Exchange essays with a classmate. Using the scoring guide for Development on page 217, score your partner's essay (while he or she scores yours). Focus on the development of ideas and use of language conventions. If necessary, rewrite your essay to improve the development and/or your use of language.

Exercise VI

English Practice

Identifying Sentence Errors

Identify the errors in the following sentences. Choose the answer that fixes the error. If the sentence contains no error, select NO CHANGE.

1. If Janine's sweater <u>was made of</u> better material, it wouldn't have frayed so easily.
    A. NO CHANGE
    B. was to be made of
    C. were made of
    D. has been made of

2. Jenna always argues with her dad because they never <u>agree to each other</u> about anything.
    F. NO CHANGE
    G. agree to one another
    H. agree together
    J. agree with each other

3. Fishermen must handle bait very carefully because <u>you could get stuck</u> on the hook.
    A. NO CHANGE
    B. you can get stuck
    C. they can get stuck
    D. he might get stuck

4. The <u>most perfect ending</u> of the well-publicized movie we attended was a great surprise to us.
    F. NO CHANGE
    G. perfect ending
    H. perfect end
    J. most perfectly

5. <u>My advise to you</u> is to go down to the police station and surrender before this gets any more complicated.
    A. NO CHANGE
    B. Some advise to you
    C. My advice to you
    D. My advice to you:

Improving Sentences

The underlined portion of each sentence below contains some flaw. Select the answer that best corrects the flaw.

6. Mental illness is diverse and complicated not only <u>to analyze but for assessing.</u>
   - A. to assess and for analysis.
   - B. to analyze but also to assess.
   - C. for assessing but also to analyze.
   - D. for analysis but also to assess.

7. The basic disagreement behind all court cases <u>are usually the same.</u>
   - F. is always the same.
   - G. are similar.
   - H. is usually the same.
   - J. are never the same.

8. <u>Singers may dislike certain song lyrics, but that doesn't prove they are good or bad.</u>
   - A. Singers dislike using lyrics in songs but that doesn't prove they are good or bad.
   - B. Even though singers disapprove of song lyrics, they sing them, good or bad.
   - C. A singer's dislike for certain song lyrics does not prove that the lyrics are good or bad.
   - D. Certain song lyrics are good or bad, but some singers may dislike them.

9. <u>The football team in their new uniforms, as well as the cheerleaders, and the exciting band music.</u>
   - F. The football team and the cheerleaders were in their new uniforms, and the band music was exciting.
   - G. The cheerleaders, the football team, and the band music was exciting in their new uniforms.
   - H. The band music was exciting as well as the football team in their new uniforms as well as the cheerleaders.
   - J. In their new uniforms as well as the cheerleaders and the exciting band music.

10. <u>The landlord denied the many charges that had been made against him, quickly and emphatically.</u>
    - A. Quickly and emphatically, the many charges that had been made against the landlord were denied.
    - B. The many charges that had been made against the landlord quickly and emphatically, were denied.
    - C. Quickly and emphatically, he denied many charges had been made against the landlord.
    - D. The landlord quickly and emphatically denied the many charges that had been made against him.

Vocabulary
Power Plus
for the
ACT
Vocabulary,
Reading, and Writing
Exercises for High Scores

Lesson Fourteen

1. **catalyst** (kat´ əl ist) *n.* a person, thing, or agent that speeds up or stimulates a result, reaction, or change
    The atom bomb was the master *catalyst* in ending World War II.
    syn: mechanism; vehicle; means

2. **jargon** (jär´ gən) *n.* vocabulary distinctive to a particular group of people
    Joe heard the attorneys exchanging legal *jargon*, but he understood little of it.
    syn: terminology; lingo

3. **judicious** (jōō dish´ əs) *adj.* showing sound judgment
    A *judicious* manager avoids favoritism and treats everyone the same way.
    syn: sensible; wise; careful   *ant: foolish; impractical; prejudicial*

4. **foible** (foi´ bəl) *n.* a minor weakness in character
    The chef's only *foible* was her forgetfulness.
    syn: fault; shortcoming

5. **benediction** (ben i dik´ shən) *n.* the act of blessing
    We bowed our heads for the *benediction* before singing the closing hymn.
    ant: curse; malediction

6. **frivolous** (friv´ ə ləs) *adj.* trivial; silly
    They wasted time arguing over a *frivolous* matter.
    syn: inconsequential; vain   *ant: vital; important*

7. **alacrity** (ə lak´ ri tē) *n.* liveliness; willingness; eagerness
    He performed his chores with *alacrity* and finished them before noon.
    syn: enthusiasm; readiness; zeal   *ant: slowness; reluctance*

8. **deify** (dē´ ə fī) *v.* to make a god of; to look upon or worship as a god
    He *deified* her, but he soon discovered that she was as human as anyone else.
    syn: idolize; worship   *ant: abhor; detest*

9. **carnage** (kär´ nij) *n.* bloody and extensive slaughter
    United Nations forces were deployed to end the *carnage* in the war-torn nation.
    syn: bloodshed; slaughter

10. **impel** (im pel´) *v.* push into motion
    Thoughts of dying thirst *impelled* him to continue walking along the desert highway.
    syn: urge; force; propel; drive　　　　　*ant: restrain*

11. **epitaph** (ep´ i taf) *n.* an inscription on a tombstone; a brief comment about a deceased person
    The tombstone had the simple *epitaph*, "Rest In Peace."

12. **harp** (härp) *v.* to persist in talking continuously (on or about something)
    My parents *harp* on the importance of completing homework.
    syn: ramble; complain

13. **lateral** (lat´ ər əl) *adj.* of or relating to the side
    Bill made a *lateral* career move by taking a new job with no change in salary.
    syn: sideways

14. **pallid** (pal´ id) *adj.* pale; faint in color
    The patient's *pallid* face and labored breathing concerned the doctor.
    syn: colorless　　　　　*ant: hearty; robust*

15. **impetuous** (im pech´ ōō əs) *adj.* acting suddenly without thought
    Impetuous behavior can be hazardous to your health.
    syn: impulsive; rash　　　　　*ant: planned; careful*

Exercise I

Words in Context

From the list below, supply the words needed to complete the paragraph. Some words will not be used.

frivolous	impetuous	deify	catalyst
foible	harp	alacrity	

1. Steve never realized it, but his single _____ was his _____ in complaining about _____ things that do not even bother most people; for example, if a waiter brought Steve the wrong beverage, Steve _____ on the mistake for days. Luckily, he was not so _____ as to cause embarrassing scenes in public.

From the list below, supply the words needed to complete the paragraph. Some words will not be used.

deify	**jargon**	**epitaph**	**harp**
carnage	**pallid**	**impel**	

2. Bonnie was an apprentice, so she didn't understand all the archaeological _____ spoken around the dig site; however, she did understand the theories as to what the farmer had discovered. Statues found near an altar suggested that the ancient tribe used to _____ certain animals and worship them in ceremonies. A large number of fractured skeletal remains at the dig site suggested that the tribe was also particularly violent; Bonnie's face grew _____ when she paused to think about the _____ that had taken place at the ancient site. The remains of hundreds of people lay in the sacrificial pit without a single marker or _____ to mark their resting place.

From the list below, supply the words needed to complete the paragraph. Some words will not be used.

benediction	**judicious**	**foible**	**catalyst**
lateral	**impel**	**alacrity**	

3. Lynn never enjoyed working in the family business, but she was the _____ responsible for transforming the company's _____ moves into huge profit margins. For years, she had spoken of leaving the business, hoping that the threat would _____ her father to seek a good replacement for her, but he never did. At the company dinner one evening, shortly after the _____, Lynn announced that she had been offered a job with a larger company at twice her current salary. To Lynn's surprise, her father congratulated her and complimented her for making a[n] _____ decision.

Exercise II

Sentence Completion

Complete the sentence in a way that shows you understand the meaning of the italicized vocabulary word.

1. Since you made an *impetuous* remark to the restaurant manager, I don't want to...

2. Too much *lateral* stress on the telephone pole caused it to...

3. They could not read the *epitaph* because...

4. Few could imagine the *carnage* that had taken place at...

5. For summer help at the factory, the boss wanted teenagers with the *alacrity* to...

6. After the reverend gave the *benediction*, everyone at the banquet...

7. The broker made a series of *judicious* investments that...

8. The new quarterback was the *catalyst* for the team's...

9. Pat's face turned *pallid* when...

10. Ken put on headphones because he could no longer stand to hear Mike *harp* about...

11. The onset of war *impelled* many people to...

12. The ancient civilization *deified* their priests; regular citizens were not even allowed to...

13. The used car was as ugly in color as it was in shape, but these were only *frivolous* concerns to Clint because he...

14. Though the billionaire gives millions to charity each year, many people refuse to look beyond his odd *foible* of...

15. You should become familiar with nautical *jargon* if you plan to...

Exercise III

Roots, Prefixes, and Suffixes

Study the entries and answer the questions that follow.

The roots *stru* and *struct* mean "to build."
The roots *tempor* and *temper* mean "time."
The root *therm* means "heat."

1. *Using literal translations as guidance, define the following words without using a dictionary.*

    A. thermostat   D. destruct
    B. instrument   E. structure
    C. hypothermia   F. contemporary

2. A *thermometer* measures _____. If you want your coffee to retain its heat, then you might put it in a[n] _____. A branch of science that deals with the study of heat is called _____-dynamics.

3. A[n] _____ worker is hired for a limited time only. In science fiction, a disruption in time might be described as a[n] _____ disturbance.

4. List as many words as you can think of that contain the roots *tempor, temper, stru,* and *struct.*

Exercise IV

Inference

Complete the sentences by inferring information about the italicized word from its context.

1. Penny didn't demonstrate the *alacrity* to play soccer, so the coach...

2. Hearing an exciting account about discovering lost treasure might *impel* an inspired listener to...

3. If the boss tells the workmen to ignore any *frivolous* concerns and simply get the job done, then the boss doesn't want the workers to worry about...

Exercise V

Critical Reading

Below is a reading passage followed by several multiple-choice questions similar to the ones you will encounter on the ACT. Carefully read the passage and choose the best answer for each of the questions.

The U.S. Fish and Wildlife Service operates the Fisheries Program and has been in existence for over 100 years. Some of the issues that inspired the program's creation are still being addressed today.

1   Americans love fish. We catch them for food, for recreation, and for income. We photograph them, we display them on walls, and we watch them in aquariums. We pursue fish in pristine wilderness and in crowded urban waters; however, habitat degradation, pollution, dams, competition from invasive species, and over-harvesting threaten America's vital aquatic resource.

2   At one time, America's pristine waters supported plentiful and robust fisheries. Our nation's natural treasures appeared to be unlimited until the Industrial Revolution and population surge required vast quantities of natural resources, notably water, timber, minerals, and wildlife. During this period, water quality and fish resources endured a rapid decline.

3   By the mid-1800s, fishermen identified the decrease in fish populations. In 1871, Spencer Fullerton Baird, Assistant Secretary of the Smithsonian Institution, wrote to Congress urging Federal protection for the nation's fisheries. Baird warned that America would lose fish as a way of life and lifestyle, and that such a calamity would leave a series of evils in its wake.

4   In response to threatened fish populations, Congress created the Commission on Fish and Fisheries, which is now called the U.S. Fish and Wildlife Service (FWS). It was the first federal agency dedicated to the conservation of natural resources. The first objective of the commission was to determine whether fisheries had indeed declined and to plot an appropriate course of action.

5   The present Fish and Wildlife Service still upholds the mission to restore our fisheries by surveying populations and habitats, raising native fish and other species, and restoring habitats to meet the goals of fisheries management plans. To fulfill these far-reaching objectives, the Fish and Wildlife Service maintains a network of field stations across the country, including seventy hatcheries and one genetics laboratory.

6   One of the most important objectives of the Fish and Wildlife Service is to moderate declining native fish populations by restoring and protecting habitats and reintroducing fish where appropriate. The FWS also works to recover species listed under the Endangered Species Act by monitoring and evaluating fish populations. Using databases, the FWS conducts long term monitoring to track the health and relative abundance of fish resources; the recorded data can then be used to create the appropriate protective measures to sustain specific ecosystems.

7   In the area of habitat conservation and management, the Fish and Wildlife Service determines habitat needs for fish populations and identifies necessary improvements. Because dams and other man-made barriers threaten many fish populations, the program works with other federal, state, and local agencies to advocate high water quality and availability of passage in streams and rivers.

8   The Fish and Wildlife Service also provides leadership in the development and application of state-of-the-art science and technology for conservation of fish and other aquatic species. Fish health centers inspect hatchery fish for pathogens, diagnose diseases, and then recommend remedial treatments to improve fish health management. Some wild fish, such as the endangered Pacific salmon, require close health monitoring to ensure their recovery. This monitoring also prevents species from becoming threatened or endangered.

9   The Fish and Wildlife Service is a government organization, but that does not mean that it interacts exclusively with other government agencies. It is currently working in partnership with Native American Tribal Nations to restore fish and wildlife, thereby improving capacity for fishing and hunting. Cooperation between the Fish and Wildlife Service and the White Mountain Apache Tribe, for example, has already been successful in recovering the once-endangered Apache trout. The trout is now on the threatened list instead of on the endangered list, and the improvement indicates that the trout and its habitat are almost fully restored.

10   Our American heritage includes a rich history of recreational fishing, and the Fish and Wildlife Service helps ensure its future. In the Southeast alone, the FWS releases more than six million fish in an attempt to enhance sport-fishing opportunities and to mitigate the negative impact of federal dams.

11   Despite a century of progress, America's fish are still in danger. The Fish and Wildlife Service is more important than ever as aquatic habitats decline due to erosion, sedimentation, altered stream flows, dams, obstructions, pollution, and invasive species. Through diligent application of sound science, effective management practices, and dedicated partnerships, the Fish and Wildlife Service will continue to conserve species and their habitats and thus ensure the future of America's fishing tradition.

1. Which of the following best describes the main idea of the passage?
   A. Fishing is an American national pastime, thanks to wildlife management.
   B. Industrialization has reduced the fish population in the United States.
   C. The Fish and Wildlife Service is dedicated to conserving fish and their habitats.
   D. The nation's water quality has declined.

2. As used in paragraph 3, *fisheries* most nearly means
   F. places in which fish are raised by people.
   G. places in which fish are stored.
   H. places in which fish are caught.
   J. coastal fishing regions.

3. Which of the following events led to a decline in fish population?
   A. the Industrial Revolution
   B. the Civil War
   C. illegal fishing practices
   D. acidic water conditions due to mine drainage

4. According to the passage, which of the following is *not* a technique used by the Fish and Wildlife Service to restore fisheries?
   F. surveying populations
   G. restoring habitats
   H. predicting pollution trends
   J. raising native fish

5. The author notes that the Fish and Wildlife Service helps the White Mountain Apache Tribe, which shows
   A. the tribe's food supply was vanishing.
   B. the Apache trout is the most popular sport fish in the United States.
   C. the agency also works with groups outside the government.
   D. the tribe will convince Congress to allocate more funds to the Fish and Wildlife Service.

6. According to the passage, which answer lists the terms in the order of best to worst?
   F. extinct, threatened, endangered
   G. endangered, extinct, threatened
   H. threatened, extinct, endangered
   J. threatened, endangered, extinct

7. Which of the following is *not* a present danger to fish habitats?
   A. sport fishing
   B. sediment in water supplies
   C. the rerouting of waterways
   D. dam building

8. Which of the following best describes the tone of the passage?
   F. thoughtful and optimistic
   G. droll and witty
   H. scholarly and substantial
   J. dry and unemotional

9. Which of the following would be an appropriate title for this passage?
    A. Native and Aquatic Nuisance Species
    B. Leadership in Aquatic Natural Science
    C. Preserving America's Fisheries
    D. U.S. Fishery Resources

10. This passage would most likely be found in a/an
    F. encyclopedia.
    G. popular fishing newsletter.
    H. science textbook.
    J. newspaper.

Level Nine

Vocabulary
Power Plus
for the ACT
Vocabulary,
Reading, and Writing
Exercises for High Scores

REVIEW
Lessons 8–14

Exercise I

Sentence Completion

Choose the best pair of words to complete the sentence. Most choices will fit grammatically and will even make sense logically, but you must choose the pair that best fits the idea of the sentence.

1. The most apparent _____ of the characters in the historical film was the presence of _____ in the dialog; for example, the medieval prince once said, "That's so cool!"
   A. minion, gaits
   B. foible, anachronisms
   C. jargon, lackeys
   D. catalyst, emissaries
   E. lament, effrontery

2. A _____ of radioactive isotopes descended upon Chernobyl after the reactor exploded, rendering the once-thriving area a _____, uninhabitable ghost town.
   A. pall, desolate
   B. demise, futile
   C. homily, frivolous
   D. catalyst, lethal
   E. kindred, martial

3. Madeline's _____ neighbor _____ interest while Madeline spoke, waiting for the chance to offer her own clever reply.
   A. rancid, careened
   B. elite, fawned
   C. nefarious, gaped
   D. blatant, deified
   E. narcissistic, feigned

4. A leaking tank of kerosene proved to be the _____ that turned a small blaze at the lighthouse into a raging _____.
    A. catalyst, holocaust
    B. carnage, fracas
    C. lampoon, genesis
    D. foible, havoc
    E. deluge, bane

5. Those citizens who were poor feared that the _____ enjoyed by the prosperous nation would _____ a generation in which no one would know the value of hard work and sacrifice.
    A. granary, impel
    B. pall, lament
    C. decadence, beget
    D. choleric, educe
    E. calumny, harp

6. The veteran golfers immediately pegged Lisa as a(n) _____ to the sport because she didn't know what was meant by bogies, birdies, or most other _____ of the game.
    A. minion, modicum
    B. neophyte, jargon
    C. beneficiary, epitaph
    D. lackey, aplomb
    E. patrician, garble

7. A(n) _____ sent to meet the hostile army was ordered by the king to _____ about the strength of his own army so that his kingdom appeared less vulnerable.
    A. benediction, query
    B. modicum, dawdle
    C. facade, harp
    D. nemesis, embroil
    E. emissary, prevaricate

8. The reality of certain starvation was enough to _____ the castaway to _____ a raft to leave the island.
    A. berated, query
    B. eradicated, educe
    C. impel, fabricated
    D. festered, beget
    E. catalyst, emit

Exercise II

Crossword Puzzle

Use the clues to complete the crossword puzzle. The answers consist of vocabulary words from lessons 8 through 14.

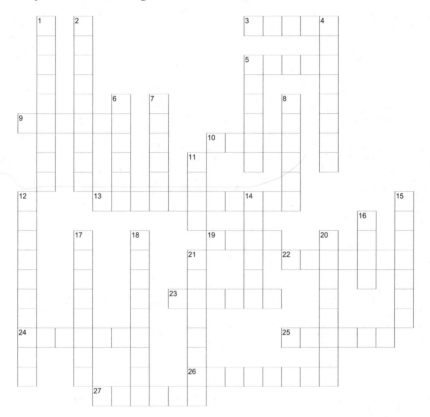

Across
3. push into motion
5. to pretend
9. useless; pointless
10. feeling of uneasiness
13. one who receives benefits
19. something that covers or conceals
22. no longer in existence
23. slavish follower
24. to draw into a fight
25. minor weakness in character
26. beginner
27. to stop

Down
1. acting suddenly without thought
2. associate; partner
4. to become weak; to lose strength
5. loud quarrel
6. to scold or rebuke
7. to hinder, obstruct
8. sermon
11. manner of walking
12. shameless boldness
14. to hint at
15. warlike; military
16. cause of ruin
17. easily angered
18. trivial; silly
20. emotionally excessive
21. glaringly bad; outrageous

Level Nine

Vocabulary
Power Plus
for the
ACT
Vocabulary,
Reading, and Writing
Exercises for High Scores

Lesson Fifteen

1. **adjunct** (aj´ ungkt) *adj.* connected or attached to in a dependent,
   subordinate, or auxiliary manner, but not a part of
   Dr. Jones, who teaches only one class, is an *adjunct* faculty member at the
   university, not a full professor.

2. **macabre** (mə kȧb´) *adj.* horrible; grim
   The *macabre* paintings featured torture scenes from the Spanish Inquisition.
   syn: ghastly; sinister   *ant: beautiful; lovely*

3. **farcical** (fär´ si kəl) *adj.* absurd; ridiculously clumsy
   The botched bank robbery became *farcical* when the getaway car broke down.
   syn: ludicrous; funny   *ant: somber; serious*

4. **debonair** (deb ə nâr´) *adj.* carefree and self-confident in manner;
   elegant and gracious
   I expected to see an awkward young man, but instead I saw a *debonair* gentleman.
   syn: charming; refined; suave   *ant: gauche; awkward*

5. **penchant** (pen´ chənt) *n.* a strong liking
   She had a *penchant* for tiny, nervous dogs with high-pitched barks.
   syn: fondness; inclination; taste   *ant: dislike; abhorrence*

6. **deplete** (di plēt´) *v.* to use up gradually
   If we *deplete* our limited food supply, we will have to hunt for food.
   syn: empty; exhaust   *ant: replenish*

7. **chicanery** (shi kā´ nə rē) *n.* the use of tricks or clever talk to deceive
   or evade
   The con artist used old-fashioned *chicanery* to steal credit card information.
   syn: trickery; subterfuge   *ant: honesty*

8. **feisty** (fī´ stē) *adj.* aggressive; lively; energetic
   The tiger cub was small but *feisty*, so we approached him with caution.
   syn: spirited; frisky   *ant: lethargic*

9. **mitigate** (mit´ i gāt) *v.* to make less severe; to become milder
   Gary put plywood over the windows to *mitigate* any damage that the
   hurricane might do to his house.
   syn: diminish; alleviate   *ant: aggravate; exacerbate*

10. **gull** (gul) *v.* to cheat; to fool or hoax
    The man in the carnival booth *gulled* me out of twenty dollars.
    syn: dupe; scam; trick

11. **nadir** (nā´ dər) *n.* lowest point
    Getting fired was the *nadir* of Bob's terrible week.
    syn: bottom   *ant: peak; zenith*

12. **equivocal** (i kwiv´ ə kəl) *adj.* ambiguous; intentionally vague
    His answer was *equivocal*, despite my plea for a simple "Yes" or "No."
    syn: uncertain; cryptic   *ant: certain; definite*

13. **genealogy** (jē nē al´ ə jē) *n.* family history
    The family tree depicted his *genealogy*.
    syn: lineage

14. **impervious** (im pûr´ vē əs) *adj.* incapable of being affected
    The wounded soldier, apparently *impervious* to pain, continued to fight.
    syn: resistant; invulnerable   *ant: vulnerable*

15. **filial** (fil´ ē əl) *adj.* of, relating to, or befitting a son or daughter
    They were not related, but Sam had a *filial* respect for his mentor.

Exercise I

Words in Context

From the list below, supply the words needed to complete the paragraph. Some words will not be used.

deplete	feisty	equivocal	gull
mitigate	chicanery	filial	

1. In an effort to _____ costs, the Lockwoods hired their neighbor, Bob, to install a new roof on their house. When Bob, a carpenter, had heard that the Lockwoods needed a new roof on their house, he advised them not to let some contractor _____ them into paying for something they -didn't need. The existing roof needed only a simple repair, Bob said, and there was no need for the Lockwoods to _____ their savings for unnecessary construction. Bob knew that some so-called discount contractors frequently used _____ and _____ estimates to cheat clients.

From the list below, supply the words needed to complete the paragraph. Some words will not be used.

feisty	debonair	chicanery	genealogy
nadir	penchant	farcical	

2. Oscar Wilde's _____ for satire shows in his play, The Importance of Being Earnest. This energetic play is a[n] _____ comedy in which _____ characters depict the expectedly refined, _____ members of the Victorian upper class as clumsy, erratic fools. At the end of the play, the two central characters, who are friends, discover that they share the same _____ and that they are actually brothers.

From the list below, supply the words needed to complete the paragraph. Some words will not be used.

mitigate	macabre	adjunct	farcical
impervious	filial	nadir	

3. Frank thought that a camping trip might be a good way to improve his _____ standing with his son and daughter, whom he rarely saw due to his long work hours. He planned a hike through the _____ of a canyon and then picked out a nice spot on the map where they could pitch tents for the night and tell _____ stories around the campfire. Frank thought that the kids would jump at the idea; unfortunately, they did not.

    "Dad," moaned Tim, "you know that I'm busy this weekend." Frank looked as if he were listening to his son, but he was actually _____ to the protest.

    "Oh, come on," said Frank, automatically. "We'll have a great time. I used to be a[n] _____ counselor for a camp—"

    "A *basketball* camp," interrupted Lisa. "And everyone knows that basketball camps are exactly where people go to learn wilderness survival skills."

Exercise II

Sentence Completion

Complete the sentence in a way that shows you understand the meaning of the italicized vocabulary word.

1. One *macabre* room at the haunted house contained…

2. The *debonair* hero of the novel waltzed right into the villain's hideout and…

3. If we *deplete* the Earth's natural resources too soon, the world will…

4. Bill broke his arm when the *feisty* horse…

5. Police put out a warning for a man who *gulls* people by claiming to be…

6. Tony's *equivocal* answer to our question only caused…

7. After years of being the new kid at school, Dawn became *impervious* to…

8. Janice is a full-time writer, but in the evenings, she is an *adjunct* instructor at…

9. Barbara was tired of watching *farcical* movies, so she decided…

10. Mary-Ellen had a *penchant* for the outdoors, so for her vacation, she…

11. The used-car salesman sometimes used *chicanery* to…

12. One way to *mitigate* the swelling of a sprained ankle is to…

13. During the *nadir* of her career, Tina…

14. The chart in the history book shows the *genealogy* of…

15. On the frontier, if parents had to leave their homestead, it was a *filial* duty for the children to…

Exercise III

Roots, Prefixes, and Suffixes

Study the entries and answer the questions that follow.

The suffix *ion* means "the act of."
The root *cret* means "to separate," "to decide," or "to distinguish."
The root *spir* means "to breathe."

1. *Using literal translations as guidance, define the following words without using a dictionary.*

    A. secretary   D. spirit
    B. excrete   E. conspire
    C. secretion   F. inspiration

2. The government might mark certain information as being _____ to distinguish it from ordinary information. People who have the special information must use _____ in deciding who receives it, because a leak could compromise national security.

3. Someone who needs help breathing might use a[n] _____. A story that breathes life into you might be said to _____ you.

4. List as many words as you can think of that contain the suffix *ion*.

Exercise IV

Inference

Complete the sentences by inferring information about the italicized word from its context.

1. If you have a *penchant* for working with children because they like to learn, then you might...

2. Two extra lodgers during the winter in the mountains might cause you to *deplete* your food supply quickly, so before winter, you should...

3. If the prisoner appears to be *impervious* to rehabilitation, the parole board will probably...

Exercise V

Writing

Here is a writing prompt similar to the one you will find on the essay writing portion of the ACT.

> Many cities and counties throughout the United States have instituted a program known as teen court, or youth court, wherein juvenile offenders who have already been found guilty of minor offenses or misdemeanors, are sentenced by juries of their peers. Interestingly, the sentences recommended by juries of teenagers are said to be harsher than the typical sentences delivered by adult judges. Are youth courts more effective than regular adult courts?
>
> Imagine that your county is planning to institute a youth court and that you are a member of the county legislature. Prepare a speech either in favor of teen court or against it. Support your argument with three reasons comprised of your experiences, observations, reading, or reasoning.

Thesis: Write a one-sentence response to the assignment. Make certain this single sentence offers a clear statement of your position.

> *Example: Youth court is a bad idea because the people doing the sentencing have no experience with the law.*

_____

_____

Organizational Plan: List at least three subtopics you will use to support your main idea. This list is your outline.

1. _____

2. _____

3. _____

Draft: Following your outline, write a good first draft of your essay. Remember to support all your points with examples, facts, references to reading, etc.

Review and Revise: Exchange essays with a classmate. Using the scoring guide for Sentence Formation and Variety on page 219, score your partner's essay (while he or she scores yours). Focus on the sentence structure and use of language conventions. If necessary, rewrite your essay to improve the sentence structure and/or your use of language.

Exercise VI

English Practice

Improving Paragraphs

Read the following passage and then choose the best revision for the underlined portions of the paragraph. The questions will require you to make decisions regarding the revision of the reading selection. Some revisions are not of actual mistakes, but will improve the clarity of the writing.

[1]

(1) The thunderhead, with <u>it's</u>[1] spires reaching miles into the evening sky, cast a shadowy curtain on the shoreline as the sun settled below the opposite horizon. (2) Helios retreated from Poseidon, and for good reason: the approaching <u>fend</u>[2] was quite possibly the largest tempest to strike the grainy shore in months.

1. A. NO CHANGE
   B. its'
   C. its
   D. it is

2. F. NO CHANGE
   G. friend
   H. find
   J. fiend

[2]

(3) Torrential rain followed the hail. (4) The sand in and near the beach became <u>so saturated with water that streams formed among</u>[3] the weeds and occasionally washed creatures out onto the open beach. (5) Few were able to cling to the sand after one pass of the <u>surged</u>[4] seawater.

3. A. NO CHANGE
   B. saturated so that streams formed among
   C. so saturated with water. Streams formed among
   D. so water saturated that streams of water formed among

4. F. NO CHANGE
   G. surging
   H. surgical
   J. surge

[3]

(6) The number of scuttling beach residents diminished with the last few rays of light. (7) Most of them were scavengers seeking food scraps from decaying horseshoe crabs, only vaguely aware that something bad approached their community. (8) They made clicking noises as they scurried across the wet sand, over the dunes, and into the tall grass, where it burrowed to hide from the pending onslaught. (9) Storms like this were known to cause flash floods. (10) Those near the water simply disappeared into the rising surf; <u>not none</u>[5] reappeared in the frothing brine that each wave carried farther inland. (11) A flock of noisy seagulls concluded their hour-long battle over a wet fast-food bag and allowed the gales to carry them inland, where they huddled beneath the joists of condemned homes and the rafters of corrugated warehouses. (12) They sat silent and inert, as though <u>their</u>[6] instinct to overcome hunger for safety had turned them into an entirely different species. (13) Unlike the rest of the beach life, the birds were safe of the storm.

5. A. NO CHANGE
   B. not any
   C. not one
   D. none never

6. F. NO CHANGE
   G. there
   H. they're
   J. they are

7. Which choice corrects the grammatical error in sentence 8?
   A. Replace *where it burrowed* with *where they burrowed.*
   B. Replace *they* with *horseshoe crabs.*
   C. Replace the comma after *grass* with a semicolon.
   D. Delete *across.*

8. Which of the following best improves the underlined portion of sentence 13?

   Unlike the rest of the beach life, <u>the birds were safe of the storm</u>.

   F. the birds were saved from the storm.
   G. the birds were safe.
   H. the birds would be saved from the storm.
   J. the birds were safer.

9. Which change would best make paragraph 3 easier to read?
   A. Exchange paragraph 3 with paragraph 5.
   B. Include more descriptions of seagulls.
   C. Begin a new paragraph after sentence 10.
   D. Begin a new paragraph after sentence 11.

[4]

(14) All but the simplest order of creatures experienced panic when the first wave of hailstones tore through vegetation and <u>through</u>[10] sand from miniature impact craters. (15) The icy projectiles, some the size of apples, stung the <u>backs'</u>[11] of exposed wildlife huddled in the grass. (16) <u>The more smaller</u>[12] crustaceans did not fare as well; hail smashed exoskeletons and leg joints. (17) They would become food for their neighbors after the storm.

10.F. NO CHANGE
   G. threw
   H. thorough
   J. though

12.F. NO CHANGE
   G. The most smaller
   H. The more smallest
   J. Smaller

11.A. NO CHANGE
   B. backs
   C. back's
   D. reverse

[5]

(18) The worst of the storm lasted only minutes, but it eliminated all but a fraction of the beach colony. (19) Most had been swept into the dark abyss beneath the starless void, and, in their <u>literally</u>[13] short lives, they would never be able to battle the riptide to return to the sands on which they spent their lives before the storm. (20) Those left in the open, disoriented from tumbling in the surf, would become food for the cackling gang of seagulls when it retuned to continue its feeding frenzy.

13.A. NO CHANGE
   B. virtually
   C. practically
   D. relatively

15.If the passage had to be shortened, which sentence could be removed without harming the intent of the passage?
   A. sentence 6
   B. sentence 7
   C. sentence 8
   D. sentence 9

14.What change would improve the chronological order of the paragraphs?
   F. Exchange paragraphs 1 and 2.
   G. Exchange paragraphs 2 and 3.
   H. Place paragraph 2 to follow paragraph 4.
   J. Place paragraph 1 to follow paragraph 4.

Level Nine

Vocabulary
Power Plus
for the **ACT**
Vocabulary,
Reading, and Writing
Exercises for High Scores

Lesson Sixteen

1. **daub** (dôb) *v.* to paint coarsely or unskillfully
Painting requires patience and consistency; you cannot simply *daub* the wood with a paint-laden brush.
syn: smear

2. **admonish** (ad mon´ ish) *v.* to warn; to caution in counsel
The lifeguard *admonished* the children for swimming beyond the buoys.
syn: advise; notify; warn

3. **obeisance** (ō bā´ səns) *n.* a bow or similar gesture expressing deep respect
The villager rendered *obeisance* as the king's entourage passed.

4. **cache** (kash) *n.* a concealed store of goods or valuables
While the campers were canoeing, bears raided their *cache* of food.
syn: hoard; reserve

5. **affliction** (ə flik´ shən) *n.* anything causing great suffering
Heatstroke can be a lethal *affliction* if not treated.
syn: difficulty; pain; burden　　　　　　　　*ant: relief; aid*

6. **mendicant** (men´ di kənt) *n.* a beggar
The tourists tried to avoid the *mendicants* sitting in front of the gift shop.

7. **aphorism** (af´ ə riz əm) *n.* a concise statement of a truth or principle
My father lives by the *aphorism,* "Waste not, want not."
syn: adage; maxim; saying

8. **oscillate** (os´ ə lāt) *v.* to swing or move back and forth like a pendulum.
Your opinion of the movie will probably *oscillate* from good to bad until you have more time to think about it.
syn: vacillate; fluctuate; alternate

9. **delete** (di lēt´) *v.* to take out; to remove
You can *delete* the third sentence because it is unnecessary.
syn: erase; cancel　　　　　　　　*ant: include; add*

10. **oust** (oust) *v.* to drive out; expel; deprive
The bailiff *ousted* the noisy courtroom spectators.
syn: eject

11. **impermeable** (im pûr´ mē ə bəl) *adj.* not permitting passage (especially of fluids)
The parka has an *impermeable* layer that keeps you dry.
syn: impenetrable; impervious   *ant: permeable*

12. **paean** (pē´ an) *n.* a fervent expression, or song, of joy or praise
The book is simply a *paean* to the candidate; it lists his achievements, but not his failures.
syn: acclaim; tribute

13. **imperturbable** (im pər tûr´ bə bəl) *adj.* not easily excited, even under pressure
The captain's *imperturbable* manner during the storm reassured the worried sailors.
syn: collected; unflustered

14. **lax** (laks) *adj.* careless or negligent
Don't become too *lax* in your studies, or you'll fail.
syn: slack; neglectful   *ant: careful; meticulous*

15. **palpable** (pal´ pə bəl) *adj.* obvious; capable of being touched or felt
The fear in the room was so *palpable* that Tim thought he could taste it.
syn: evident; conspicuous   *ant: obscure; unclear*

Exercise I

Words in Context

From the list below, supply the words needed to complete the paragraph. Some words will not be used.

admonish	affliction	lax	imperturbable
delete	obeisance	oust	

1. Everyone knew that Kiplar was an outsider when he failed to show proper _____ to the passing queen. One of the royal escorts immediately spotted Kiplar and walked over to _____ him for his failure to show respect.
  "What is this _____ of yours that prevents you from taking a knee upon sight of our queen? Shall we _____ you from your sleepy village and see how you fare in a dungeon?" The guard's threat did not faze the _____ man. Kiplar, still standing, simply smiled.

From the list below, supply the words needed to complete the paragraph. Some words will not be used.

paean	aphorism	impermeable	affliction
palpable	lax	daub	

2. Justin began to have second thoughts about his summer job when the temperature rose to ninety degrees. The high humidity was more than _____. For the third day in a row, he stood on a flimsy ladder and _____ maroon paint onto the side of Mrs. Bailey's house. He wore no gloves today; yesterday, he had discovered that the cheap cotton painter's gloves were not _____ when he removed them and found his hands stained maroon. To make matters worse, Mrs. Bailey frequently came outside to ensure that Justin hadn't become _____ on the job. The old _____, "time flies when you're having fun," couldn't have been more applicable to Justin because each ten-hour day of painting felt like an eternity. If hard work builds character, thought Justin, then he should have a[n] _____ amount of character after this job.

From the list below, supply the words needed to complete the paragraph. Some words will not be used.

paean	delete	oust	mendicant
cache	oscillate	palpable	

3. In the late afternoon, Marvin opened the bottom drawer of his desk to reveal a[n] _____ of snack cakes and little bags of potato chips. He helped himself to a cream-filled cupcake as he perused old e-mail messages and _____ any old ones that were just taking up space on the computer's hard drive. A heavy fan _____ in the corner of the office, causing self-adhesive notes and thumb-tacked comic strips to flap around in the breeze every few seconds. Next to the fan was a tied trash bag full of empty aluminum soda cans for Joe, a[n] _____ who lived in the alley behind the magazine publisher. Joe, who chose the streets over shelters, inspired many people at the office, and he had no idea that Marvin's next article was going to be a[n] _____ to the homeless who have learned to sustain themselves despite their austere living conditions.

Exercise II

Sentence Completion

Complete the sentence in a way that shows you understand the meaning of the italicized vocabulary word.

1. The sprinkler head *oscillates* so that the entire lawn…

2. The book began with the old *aphorism*, "…

3. The magazine editor told the writer to *delete*…

4. A *mendicant* outside the grocery store asked me…

5. Bouncers at the club *ousted* Herbert because he…

6. The arctic explorers could not find their *cache* of supplies because…

7. If you wear boots that are *impermeable*, you won't have to worry about…

8. The *affliction* became widespread when villagers drank water from…

9. The National Anthem is a *paean* to…

10. The young student bowed his head in *obeisance* to…

11. The old, *imperturbable* dog lay on the floor and let the puppies…

12. I'll *admonish* you this time, but the next time you do it, I'm going to…

13. The *lax* worker at the power plant failed to notice that…

14. During the funeral, Amy *daubed*…

15. The admiration I feel for The Beatles is almost *palpable*; for every time I…

Exercise III

Roots, Prefixes, and Suffixes

Study the entries and answer the questions that follow.

The roots *liber* and *liver* mean "free."
The root *soph* means "wise."
The root *men* means "to think."

1. *Using literal translations as guidance, define the following words without using a dictionary.*

    A. philosophy   D. liberty
    B. sophomore   E. liberate
    C. mental   F. demented

2. A person who has lived a complex life and gathered wisdom might be described as being _____.

3. List as many words as you can think of that contain the roots *liber*, *liver*, or *men*.

Exercise IV

Inference

Complete the sentences by inferring information about the italicized word from its context.

1. If someone has an *affliction* that affects his or her legs, then that person might...

2. Pirates might hide their *cache* of stolen goods so that...

3. A security camera might be designed to *oscillate* in order to...

Exercise V

Critical Reading

Below is a reading passage followed by several multiple-choice questions similar to the ones you will encounter on the ACT. Carefully read the passage and choose the best answer for each of the questions.

The following passage discusses the Tunguska event of 1908, in which a strange object exploded with devastating force in the sky over Siberia.

1   In the quest to find answers to unexplained mysteries, there are times to be skeptical and times to be creative. The explanation of the Tunguska explosion of 1908 requires creativity, unless skeptics actually find some physical evidence.

2   On the morning of June 30th, 1908, residents near the remote Tunguska River, Siberia, witnessed what was doubtlessly the largest, unexplained cataclysmic event of the twentieth century. According to the many eyewitnesses, a blazing, white light—brighter than lightning—streaked across the sky, pulling a tail hundreds of miles in length. Suddenly, while still airborne, the mysterious object detonated over the forest, setting everything beneath it on fire and sending destructive shock waves and heat throughout a 300-mile radius. The explosion flattened every tree in the forest as far as thirteen miles from the blast, and simple mountaineers watched as homes, plants, and livestock burst into flames from a rapid surge of intense heat. Inhabitants close to the explosion were thrown through the air like rag dolls, and some of them died as a result of broken bones, severe burns, or a strange sickness that ensued in the following days. Immediately after the blast, rocks rained upon the countryside and dust filled the air, as though a volcano had blown its top. A column of fire, perhaps a mile in width, lit the sky well into the evening. The description of the ensuing fireball and mushroom cloud most nearly resembles the modern description of a nuclear explosion; however, nuclear weapons weren't even tested until 1945.

3   People had no doubt that something exploded; seismographs around the world detected shock waves that had traveled through thousands of miles of earth, and the sky over Siberia radiated an unnatural glow well into the evening. Unfortunately, due to the isolated region in which the explosion occurred, and the chaotic political state of Russia at the time, no one conducted a formal investigation of the Tunguska event until 1921. Members of the Russian Meteorological Institute found widespread damage, but they found no meteorite impact craters. The detonation had literally leveled the forest around the center of the blast, and people living in the region reported that witnesses who didn't die from heat or blast effects died instead from symptoms that indicated radiation poisoning.

4   Almost a century after the event, many scientists readily attribute the bizarre explosion to an asteroid or comet that exploded before reaching the earth. Others, including some eyewitnesses, are not so ready to assign such natural explanations

to the event; there is no impact crater at the epicenter of the explosion, and investigators discovered no fragments, large or small, of what would have been a massive meteorite. Frenzied theorists offer explanations of alien attacks, crashing spaceships, antimatter reactions, lightning from the earth, and even a disastrous test of an energy weapon built by the eccentric genius, Nikola Tesla. Serious, ongoing research points not to UFOs or low-probability natural phenomena; instead, most scientists attribute the event to an asteroid or a fragment of a comet, both of which are among the few natural objects capable of such devastating explosions.

5   The destruction caused by the Tunguska explosion is commensurate with the effects of a forty-megaton nuclear explosion—that's 1,000 times more powerful than the Hiroshima bomb. In theory, meteorites could indeed cause the massive degree of destruction, but no one is sure why (or if) a meteoroid would detonate before striking the ground.

6   The exploding comet theory is quickly gaining credibility as an explanation, because a comet made up of ice and dust would not necessarily leave the evidence required to confirm the material that made up the object. In recent years, researchers have compared the dust at the Tunguska site to the dust found in Antarctica that is known to be from meteorite impacts. The samples are very similar in composition. Scientists also report finding particles imbedded in trees around the site. The particles, they report, are also similar to meteorites in composition; however, the comet theory neglects the vast thermal destruction and the apparent radiation effects of the explosion.

7   Some Tunguska theorists offer an antimatter-annihilation as an explanation Antimatter in sufficient quantity might yield an explosion resembling that of nuclear origin, complete with the radiation effects; however, few can explain how antimatter would exist—let alone travel—throughout our galaxy without being annihilated well before reaching earth.

8   To many, the antimatter theory might be more credible than the final alternative: a UFO—a spacecraft or missile of extraterrestrial origin—exploded over Tunguska. The craft would have to have been large, of course, to cause such devastation, but without physical evidence of meteors, comets, or an antimatter annihilation, investigators cannot write off such a theory.

9   Over a century has passed since the Tunguska explosion. It is time to solve the mystery before the event occurs again, but this time in a populated area. The threat of meteorites and other extraterrestrial bodies striking earth is a growing concern for humanity; we must account for such threats in this new millennium of human existence. The next Tunguska, whether caused by meteorites, antimatter, or even UFOs, might not be so forgiving as to strike in one of the most desolate areas of the planet. If Tunguska was the product of an asteroid, then we need to prove it and create an appropriate means of defense. If Tunguska was something more complicated than an asteroid, which is quite possible, then we've a lot of reading to do and technology to develop.

1. The overall tone of the passage is best described as
    A. concerned.
    B. optimistic.
    C. apologetic.
    D. timid.

2. According to the passage, where was the object when it exploded?
    F. approximately 300 feet underground
    G. in the upper atmosphere
    H. in the air, over the forest
    J. on the forest floor

3. The explosion could not have been an atomic blast because
    A. people had no means of propulsion for nuclear weapons in 1908.
    B. there were no radiation effects among the witnesses.
    C. the Tunguska event predates nuclear testing by nearly forty years.
    D. the Russian Meteorological Institute controlled the only atomic bomb.

4. As used in paragraph 3, *seismograph* refers to
    F. an instrument that alerts people to incoming meteorites.
    G. an instrument that receives worldwide messages.
    H. an instrument that detects movement of the ground.
    J. an instrument that measures electromagnetic pulse.

5. Why, according to the passage, must humans develop technology?
    A. to defend the planet from extraterrestrial threats
    B. to better understand the properties of antimatter
    C. so that civilization can colonize other planets if necessary
    D. to prepare to survive this type of threat

6. According to paragraph 4, which two groups offer explanations of the Tunguska explosion?
    F. the Russian Meteorological Institute and the U.S. Department of State
    G. witnesses of the explosion and people on the train
    H. educated workers and local physicians
    J. overzealous thinkers and real scientists

7. Which of the following best describes the apparent strategy of the passage?
   A. The passage presents the explosion as fiction, but offers theories of the event.
   B. The passage argues in support of the atomic blast theory.
   C. The passage is intended to frighten readers.
   D. The passage presents the explosion as fact and acknowledges several theories of the event.

8. The skeptics mentioned in the passage
   F. have the support of the author.
   G. are the ultimate authority.
   H. have negative connotations.
   J. are closest to solving the mystery.

9. The skeptics mentioned in the passage would probably agree with which statement?
   A. A meteorite caused the blast.
   B. Tunguska might have been a nuclear event.
   C. Nikoli Tesla blew up Tunguska accidentally.
   D. Antimatter is to blame.

10. Choose the most appropriate title for the passage.
   F. Historic Meteorite Collisions
   G. What the Skeptics Don't Know
   H. Truth and Consequences in Tunguska
   J. The History of Tunguska

Level Nine

Vocabulary
Power Plus
for the
ACT
Vocabulary,
Reading, and Writing
Exercises for High Scores

Lesson Seventeen

1. **pariah** (pə rī′ ə) *n.* a social outcast
   He knew that he would become a *pariah* if anyone saw him in the police car.
   syn: exile; outsider   *ant: insider*

2. **fluent** (flōō′ ənt) *adj.* able to express oneself easily and clearly
   The spy travels with ease because she is *fluent* in four languages.
   syn: well-versed   *ant: inept*

3. **cavort** (kə vôrt′) *v.* to leap about in a sprightly manner; romp
   The children *cavorted* with the puppy in the back yard.
   syn: frolic; prance; caper

4. **pedagogue** (ped′ ə gog) *n.* a schoolteacher
   A single *pedagogue* taught all the children in the rural county.
   syn: educator

5. **melee** (mā′ lā) *n.* a noisy, confused fight
   By the time the police arrived, the *melee* was over.
   syn: skirmish; fracas

6. **ensue** (en sōō′) *v.* to follow as a result
   The monkey escaped from the laboratory, and an epidemic *ensued*.
   syn: to result   *ant: to cause*

7. **desecrate** (des′ i krāt) *v.* to damage a holy place; to treat with
   irreverence
   The vandals *desecrated* the little church.
   syn: vandalize; violate   *ant: consecrate*

8. **personification** (per son ə fi kā′ shən) *n.* a person or thing that
   represents an idea
   The old woman was the very *personification* of greed.

9. **bias** (bī′ əs) *n.* a prejudiced view (either for or against); a preference
   The jurors were instructed to review the facts without *bias*.
   syn: partiality; favoritism

10. **aloof** (ə lōōf´) *adj.* reserved, distant
The principal remained *aloof* for a few days after arguing with the teacher.
syn: detached; cold; remote   *ant: warm; friendly*

11. **gyrate** (jī´ rāt) *v.* to rotate or revolve quickly; to spiral
People used to dance, but now they simply *gyrate* in random patterns.
syn: revolve; whirl

12. **fiat** (fī´ at) *n.* an official order
The dictator's harsh *fiat* turned the rebels into outlaws.
syn: decree; authorization

13. **fidelity** (fi del´ i tē) *n.* faithfulness
The king told his subjects that their *fidelity* would be rewarded.
syn: loyalty; devotion   *ant: treachery*

14. **rambunctious** (ram bungk´ shəs) *adj.* unruly; uncontrollable
The *rambunctious* twins kept the house in an uproar from morning until night.
syn: wild; disorderly; boisterous   *ant: calm; pacific; tranquil*

15. **hilarity** (hi lar´ i tē) *n.* gaiety; joviality
Uncle Harvey's jokes always brought *hilarity* to the family picnics.
syn: mirth; merriment; glee   *ant: sadness; misery*

Exercise I

Words in Context

From the list below, supply the words needed to complete the paragraph. Some words will not be used.

fluent	pariah	desecrate	ensue
fiat	rambunctious	melee	

1. Community outrage _____ when the groundskeeper reported that a group of _____ teenagers had _____ the cemetery.
   "What kind of _____ sinks so low as to destroy that which cannot be defended?" asked the mayor when told of the crime. "These are memorials to our forefathers, our families." The mayor, forced to take some type of action to prevent such outrageous crimes, issued a[n] _____ mandating a curfew on the small town.

From the list below, supply the words needed to complete the paragraph. Some words will not be used.

bias	aloof	pariah	pedagogue
hilarity	cavort	fluent	

2. The aging _____, a teacher for twenty-two years, was _____ enough in adolescent psychology to know that something was wrong with Anne. The girl normally _____ in the halls and laughed with her friends, but she hadn't spoken a word in week. During class, she remained _____ and stared out the window into a distant field. The teacher's concern was without _____—he genuinely cared about all his students, not just those, like Anne, who made teaching enjoyable.

From the list below, supply the words needed to complete the paragraph. Some words will not be used.

fidelity	hilarity	melee	fiat
personification	gyrate	cavort	

3. Startled by crashing noises coming from the office, Tina ran out of the living room to find her two sons involved in a[n] _____. Apparently, they were fighting over who was next to spin around in the office chair.
    "You've got hundreds of toys upstairs, and you two fight over who gets to _____ in an office chair?" screamed Tina. "Go play outside—it's a nice day!" As the boys, one six and the other seven, ran into the yard, Tina wondered what would become the next object of conflict. Her boys were the _____ of sibling rivalry—they fought over rights to everything, no matter how silly. The ridiculous disputes were often cause for _____, but too much of it quickly became irritating. Despite the rivalry, Tina didn't question the boys' _____ to one another as brothers; they helped each other as often as they fought.

Exercise II

Sentence Completion

Complete the sentence in a way that shows you understand the meaning of the italicized vocabulary word.

1. The *hilarity* of the celebration was interrupted when...

2. Joe felt like the *pariah* of the class because he...

3. After buying new furniture, Dad warned the *rambunctious* children to...

4. Jan-Tommy is from Norway, but he became *fluent* in English by...

5. The general questioned the *fidelity* of his troops before he ordered them to...

6. Bobby *cavorted* around in the living room until his mom told him that...

7. The king issued a *fiat* which stated that his subjects were to...

8. The *pedagogue* eventually stopped teaching and became the...

9. When the young girl jumped on the table and began to *gyrate* wildly, her mother...

10 Like most action movies, this one featured a big *melee* near the end in which the hero...

11. When Cory began to act very *aloof*, his parents knew that something was wrong because he was usually...

12. Cheering *ensued* when the home team...

13. To eliminate any *bias* from the team selection, judges were chosen from a group of people who had never...

14. Tomb raiders and scavengers *desecrated* the ancient pyramid by...

15. Jerry, who missed the plane that crashed and then bought a winning lottery ticket, is the very *personification* of...

Exercise III

Roots, Prefixes, and Suffixes

Study the entries and answer the questions that follow.

The root *tract* means "to draw" or "to dig."
The root *anthro* means "man."
The suffix *ology* means "the study of."
The suffix *oid* means "like."

1. *Using literal translations as guidance, define the following words without using a dictionary.*

    A. intractable   D. zoologist
    B. contract   E. spheroid
    C. biology   F. humanoid

2. The study of man is called _____, and a creature with characteristics that resembles those of man is called a[n] _____.

3. A building *contractor* might need to _____ a foundation before beginning construction. You might find yourself drawn toward a[n] _____ person.

4. List as many words as you can think of that contain the root *tract* and the suffixes *oid* and *ology*.

Exercise IV

Inference

Complete the sentences by inferring information about the italicized word from its context.

1. If judges show *bias* in favor of a particular contestant in a beauty pageant, that contestant will probably…

2. The movie villain was described as the *personification* of evil because he…

3. Few people talked to Billy, the *pariah* of the town, because he…

Exercise V

Writing

Here is a writing prompt similar to the one you will find on the essay writing portion of the ACT.

> Because it is one of the most widely spoken languages in the world, English is often described as the world's *lingua franca*, or language used between people who do not share the same mother language.
>
> While English presently brings worlds together, it is far from becoming something so vast as a world language. English speakers number a mere 350 million, tying with the number of Spanish speakers in the world, and falling far short of China's one billion.
>
> Should there be an official world language, similar to Latin's place as the language of science? With globalization in full swing, a world language would be the primary economic mode of business of the world. English has been it since the dawn of globalization, but will it, or should it, continue in its role?
>
> What factors should decide the next *lingua franca*? Suggest which language it should be, and provide at least three reasons why that one language should take precedence over others. Support your reasons with your observations, experience, or reasoning.

Thesis: Write a one-sentence response to the assignment. Make certain this single sentence offers a clear statement of your position.

Example: The next lingua franca *should be a neutral language so that it is not biased toward one nation or another.*

_____

_____

Organizational Plan: List at least three subtopics you will use to support your main idea. This list is your outline.

1. _____

2. _____

3. _____

Draft: Following your outline, write a good first draft of your essay. Remember to support all your points with examples, facts, references to reading, etc.

Review and Revise: Exchange essays with a classmate. Using the scoring guide for Word Choice on page 220, score your partner's essay (while he or she scores yours). Focus on word choice and the use of language conventions. If necessary, rewrite your essay to improve the word choice and/or your use of language.

Exercise VI

English Practice

Identifying Sentence Errors

Identify the errors in the following sentences. Choose the answer that fixes the error. If the sentence contains no error, select NO CHANGE.

1. None of the friends in the lower apartment <u>was injured</u> when the waterbed burst through the ceiling.
   A. NO CHANGE
   B. were injured
   C. got injured
   D. are injured

2. Bring with you only necessary <u>clothes, leave</u> your blankets at home.
   F. NO CHANGE
   G. clothes; leave
   H. clothes, so leave
   J. clothes leave

3. Today, <u>less than two out of every 300</u> Americans work in the fields to produce fruits and vegetables.
   A. NO CHANGE
   B. less than 2 out of every three hundred
   C. fewer then two out of every three hundred
   D. fewer than two out of every 300

4. When I told you I had no plans for the weekend, I did not <u>mean to infer</u> that I didn't want to plan anything.
   F. NO CHANGE
   G. mean to infer to you
   H. mean to imply
   J. mean for you to imply

5. Although she admits she has never seen one, my Aunt Margaret says she <u>believes in angles</u> anyway.
   A. NO CHANGE
   B. has a belief in angles
   C. believes in angels
   D. believes, in angels,

Improving Sentences

The underlined portion of each sentence below contains some flaw. Select the answer that best corrects the flaw.

6. Doug took a nasty blow to the <u>head, but may be his condition will improve</u> after he gets a few hours of rest.
    F. head but may be his condition will improve
    G. head but maybe a few hours of rest will improve
    H. head, but maybe his condition will improve
    J. head, but his condition will improve

7. Anne walked into town hall, made some nasty remarks in front of the mayor, <u>and then she rushes right out to the bus.</u>
    A. then rushes out the door and right onto the bus.
    B. and then rushed right out to the bus.
    C. so she rushed out and gets on the bus.
    D. then she rushed right out to the bus.

8. Some women like to wear short skirts, <u>but long dresses are preferred by others.</u>
    F. whereas some do not prefer short skirts.
    G. but sometimes they only wear long dresses.
    H. and others are long-dress wearers.
    J. but others prefer long dresses.

9. <u>If our radio is turned on and up all the time and we don't do our homework properly.</u>
    A. If our radio is turned on and up all the time, we don't do our homework properly.
    B. Our homework isn't done properly and if the radio is too loud, it's on all the time.
    C. We don't do our homework properly, and the radio is on all the time and too loud.
    D. We have the radio on all the time and up too loud if we don't do our homework properly.

10. <u>Tiffany and Jeremy fought over the remote control while I tried to read a book noisily.</u>
    F. The remote control was fought over noisily by Jeremy and Tiffany while I tried to read a book.
    G. Tiffany and Jeremy fought over the remote control while I noisily tried to read a book.
    H. Tiffany and Jeremy fought noisily over the remote control while I tried to read a book.
    J. I tried to read a book noisily while Tiffany and Jeremy fought over the remote control.

Level Nine

Vocabulary
Power Plus
for the
ACT
Vocabulary,
Reading, and Writing
Exercises for High Scores

Lesson Eighteen

1. **genocide** (je´ nə sīd) *n.* the deliberate destruction of a group of people
The Nazi *genocide* of millions of Jewish people is a dark time in world history.

2. **zaftig** (zäf´ tig) *adj.* having a full, shapely figure
She knew that she was too *zaftig* to wear the little dress.
syn: curvaceous

3. **predilection** (pre dəl ek´ shən) *n.* a preference toward someone or something
His *predilection* for fast food helped to clog his arteries at an early age.
syn: preference; partiality; penchant　　　*ant: aversion; hatred*

4. **faux** (fō) *adj.* artificial; false; not genuine
The *faux*-marble countertop is really made of cheap plastic.
syn: fake; imitation　　　*ant: authentic; true*

5. **foray** (for´ ā) *n.* a surprise attack
The Green Berets conducted a *foray* on the enemy fuel depot.
syn: raid; incursion

6. **conjecture** (kən jek´ chər) *n.* a judgment or opinion based on little or questionable evidence
The defense attorney said that the prosecutor's claims were pure *conjecture*.
syn: speculation; guesswork　　　*ant: fact*

7. **allocate** (al´ ə kāt) *v.* to distribute, allot, or designate
The government *allocated* the funds for victims of natural disasters.
syn: apportion; assign

8. **gratis** (gra´ təs) *adj.* free; without charge
Tom could have earned ten dollars an hour, but he volunteered to work *gratis*.

9. **materialistic** (mə tir ē əl is´ tik) *adj.* wanting material possessions
The *materialistic* man cared only about keeping up with his neighbors.
　　　　　ant: altruistic

10. **belabor**   (bi la´ bər)   *v.*   to work at something beyond practicality; to overstress
Mom constantly *belabored* the fact that our grades would have to get us through college because her paycheck wouldn't.
syn: stress; overdo   *ant: disregard; ignore*

11. **progeny**   (prä´ jən ē)   *n.*   offspring; children
Only a few of the sea turtle's *progeny* will survive predators and live to adulthood.
syn: descendents; young   *ant: ancestors*

12. **quintessential**   (kwin tə sen´ shəl)   *adj.*   the most typical; ideal
Johann Sebastian Bach was the *quintessential* Baroque composer.
syn: model; standard

13. **rudimentary**   (rōō də men´ tə rē)   *adj.*   basic; not refined or well developed
She claimed to be a great critic despite her *rudimentary* understanding of literature.
syn: elementary; undeveloped   *ant: refined; sophisticated*

14. **monolithic**   (mä nə lith´ ik)   *adj.*   massive, uniform, and solid
The *monolithic* monument, made of pure granite, weighed one million pounds.

15. **manifesto**   (ma nə fes´ tō)   *n.*   a public declaration of policies or intentions
The conservation group's *manifesto* declared that its members were opponents of polluting industries.
syn: proclamation

Exercise I

Words in Context

From the list below, supply the words needed to complete the paragraph. Some words will not be used.

rudimentary	predilection	allocate	monolithic
conjecture	quintessential	belabor	

1. Horace attributes his career as a skyscraper window-washer to his _____ for being in high places. He also says that the _____ rule of the trade is not, "Don't look down," but, "Always attach your safety harness." Anyone with a[n] _____ knowledge of climbing knows that equipment fails and people fall if they haven't taken any precautions.

    "I can't _____ the point enough," said Horace. "Safety, safety, safety." After the brief interview, Horace climbed back into his elevator scaffold and began the ascent back to the forty-first story of the _____ building that he was cleaning this week.

From the list below, supply the words needed to complete the paragraph. Some words will not be used.

gratis	progeny	monolithic	genocide
materialistic	allocate	faux	

2. Cindy was not _____, but she still refused to buy the _____ leather furniture; she really believed that having plastic furniture was tacky. When she _____ a large portion of her savings for purchasing things for her new home, she promised herself to buy only items that would retain some of their intrinsic, if not monetary, value. The ornate furnishings that she ultimately selected would last for a long time, perhaps long enough for her _____ to enjoy. After making the substantial purchase, Cindy was happy to learn the store would deliver the items to her home _____.

From the list below, supply the words needed to complete the paragraph. Some words will not be used.

zaftig	genocide	quintessential	foray
faux	conjecture	manifesto	

3. Few outsiders knew for sure the condition of the city in the days following the violent revolution, but most _____ described a place of rampant looting and lawlessness after the rebels' _____ into the capital city. Winston, the nearest correspondent, traveled to the city to report the situation, and what he found shocked him. Poor-quality copies of the revolutionaries' _____ hung on bullet-riddled walls next to posters of a smiling, _____ woman advertising a chain of fitness clubs. Orphaned children and distraught mothers roamed the streets as remnants of the near-_____ that had occurred in the weeks leading to the uprising.

Exercise II

Sentence Completion

Complete the sentence in a way that shows you understand the meaning of the italicized vocabulary word.

1. After the accident, the *materialistic* man worried only about...

2. The ballerina eventually became too *zaftig* to...

3. You will certainly see *monolithic* structures if you go...

4. The family *allocated* a portion of its income for...

5. Every time the kids prepared to go boating, Dad *belabored* them with the importance of...

6. The world accused the ruler of *genocide* for ordering his army to...

7. The political party released a *manifesto* that described the party's...

8. Critics complained that the new book was mostly *conjecture* because it...

9. Olivia escaped the destitute nation so that her *progeny* might...

10. Sam had a *predilection* for living in the mountains, so he...

11. Yvonne's *rudimentary* knowledge of auto repair was not enough for her to...

12. During the Vikings' *foray*, the surprised villagers...

13. The *quintessential* teenager spends lots of time...

14. The *faux* mink coat is actually...

15. The club thought that the former president would deliver a speech *gratis*, but instead, he...

Exercise III

Roots, Prefixes, and Suffixes

Study the entries and answer the questions that follow.

The roots *ped* and *pod* mean "foot."
The root *phob* means "fear."
The root *port* means "to carry" or "bring."

1. *Using literal translations as guidance, define the following words without using a dictionary.*

    A. import   D. report
    B. transport   E. podiatrist
    C. impede   F. hydrophobia

2. A _____ creature has two legs, a stand with three legs is called a[n] _____, and an animal with four legs is called a[n] _____.

3. If you are afraid of feet, then you might be said to have _____. Someone who fears being in a *claustrum*, or an enclosed space, is said to have _____.

4. List as many words as you can think of that contain the roots *ped*, *pod*, and *port*.

Exercise IV

Inference

Complete the sentences by inferring information about the italicized word from its context.

1. To a *materialistic* person, owning an expensive car might be more important than...

2. The *faux* brick paneling is cheaper than real brick, but it...

3. The scientist's theory was mostly *conjecture*, so the board of directors...

Exercise V

Critical Reading

Below is a reading passage followed by several multiple-choice questions similar to the ones you will encounter on the ACT. Carefully read the passage and choose the best answer for each of the questions.

The author of the following passages discusses new trends in the antiques business.

1   Antique shops are more than just a place of business: They are museums in which the artifacts are for sale, and each item includes a fascinating history. Even antiques with unknown stories can inspire the imagination and transport customers to different eras. An old dining table might be the lone remaining witness to a special family dinner on the night before the two oldest sons enlisted in the Union army and, weeks later, died at Gettysburg. The same Victorian-era mirror that helped a woman to check the alignment of her crinolette in 1870 probably reflected images of the moon-landing on a television set in the same room in 1969. Old paintings, displayed on walls for dozens of years, could have touched the lives of countless people, perhaps in ways that significantly altered lives and, thus, the future. Dealers who have built lives around these captivating antiques are now providing ways to take the experience to new levels by providing, in addition to antiques, interior decorating services.

2   A visit to the showroom of an established antiques dealer-decorator in Reading, Pennsylvania, will reveal a two-level harlequin floor covered with eighteenth-century furniture. The walls and ceiling are loaded with corresponding period accessories: chandeliers, mirrors, china, art prints, and wall hangings. A separate room contains even more period artifacts such as columns, iron gates, and modernized lighting fixtures. Adjacent rooms in the dealership contain similar arrangements with nineteenth- and twentieth-century antiques. Most of these later artifacts qualify as Americana, and many of them are very rare or very unusual; for example, there is Native American art, furniture made from recycled cigar boxes, and a full-body stuffed moose complete with antlers.

3   Despite the array of artifacts, the largest contributing factor to the dealer's success is the arrangement of the shop itself. Furniture and accessories are displayed in the same fashion that a modern furniture company would display complete suites. Not all of the items are matched in make or origin, but the dealer applies a lifetime of expertise and good taste to ensure that items match in style, color, and period. Customers can then shop for completed arrangements of antiques, and, if they want items that the dealer does not stock, the dealer will gladly offer locating services. Dealers will also provide locating services if there is a need to find items that match a specific interior decoration design.

4   As a logical attempt to further establish and expand business, many antiques dealers now offer interior decorating services. With decades of education through experience, antiques dealers are often the authorities in total arrangement accuracy.

In addition to identifying proper furniture and accessories, dealer-decorators can recommend proper paint schemes, woodwork, masonry, carpet, and flooring to match existing homes, color schemes, and personalities. Allowing decorators to create the proper ambiance, of course, requires great confidence on behalf of buyers, but the credentialed decorator will be able to create arrangements that glow with the aura of the selected time period. Furthermore, most reputable dealers guarantee their coordination skills with their antique furnishings, which is why they are often called upon to decorate notable venues such as period houses, inns, restaurants, and hotels. Most dealers prefer to work with genuine antiques. Reproduction antiques are available, but most dealers shun them as cheap substitutes, and it seldom poses a problem because customers who can afford such decorating services can usually afford the genuine antiques as well.

5   Antiques dealer-decorators are still dealers at heart, so collectors need not worry that individual antiques will ever become scarce or too overpriced. One unchanging aspect of antique dealerships is that they all get overcrowded with artifacts at some point, and dealers solve this problem by hosting "house sales" to make room for new collections. Many dealers rent trucks or vans and take their goods to flea markets or auctions with the intention of selling every last piece of cargo. Antiques dealers like nothing better than driving home empty trucks, so it is possible to find excellent prices for what could be valuable antiques at these events. For dealers, flea markets are not just for selling antiques; at these events, dealers have the opportunity to exercise their own skills in recognizing items that would appeal to collectors. This skill ensures that dealers build effective inventories and make new customers.

6   Individual antiques can certainly be beautiful and valuable outside of a collection, but few who appreciate the intrinsic value of artifacts can quell their calling to collect more. The rewarding hobby can become quite addictive as collectors increasingly crave the craftsmanship, the distinctiveness, and even the conversational appeal that relics from past societies provide. Luckily, if collections get too large, antiques decorators can ensure that portals to previous times will be accurate, attractive places—single rooms or entire homes—in which time can stop for a while.

1.   What is the error in the first sentence?
     A. *Artifacts* is too closely related to *antiques*.
     B. *Fascinating* is too subjective.
     C. The colon should be a comma.
     D. *Plural* shops does not match singular *place*.

2.   Which is the author's intention for including the descriptions of objects in paragraph 1?
     F. to convince readers to become antiques dealers
     G. to explain why antique furniture is better than new furniture
     H. to explain the mysterious appeal of antiques
     J. to foreshadow an event later in the passage

3. In paragraph 2, the word *harlequin* probably refers to
   A. paperback romance stories.
   B. comedy.
   C. insect infested.
   D. a diamond-shaped pattern.

4. In paragraph 2, *Americana* refers to
   F. furniture made in the USA.
   G. antiques that reflect the culture of the United States.
   H. imported reproductions of American antiques.
   J. Southwest American Indian artifacts.

5. According to paragraph 3, why would an antiques dealer offer locating services?
   A. to find antiques of a lost period
   B. to find antiques to match an interior design
   C. to complete a decorating scheme
   D. to offer a particular interior design for a certain customer

6. As used in paragraph 4, *ambiance* most nearly means
   F. behavior.
   G. furnishings.
   H. atmosphere.
   J. artwork.

7. Antiques dealers handle an overstocking of inventory by
   A. offering in-store merchandise at half price.
   B. having house sales or by selling items outside their dealerships.
   C. moving everything to a special room.
   D. having a going-out-of-business sale.

8. It is important for dealers to educate themselves in recognizing items of interest to collectors because
   F. it shows expertise in pottery making, calligraphy, and basketry.
   G. it inspires new decorative schemes that attract customers.
   H. it helps successfully date artifacts and identify forgeries.
   J. it helps to build proper inventories and to please new customers.

9. Which of the following ideas does the last sentence of the passage suggest?
    A. Restored antiques last much longer than common furniture.
    B. It is beneficial to create the effect that time has slowed or stopped.
    C. Antiques decorators manipulate time for a fee.
    D. Antiques allow people to feel what people from other times felt.

10. This passage would most likely be found in a/an
    F. local business feature of a newspaper.
    G. letter to a friend.
    H. home-improvement magazine.
    J. advertising brochure.

Vocabulary
Power Plus
for the ACT
Vocabulary,
Reading, and Writing
Exercises for High Scores

Lesson Nineteen

1. **tantamount** (tan´ tə maunt) *adj.* of essentially equal value or
    significance
    To the professor, using notes during tests is *tantamount* to cheating.
    syn: equivalent; commensurate   *ant: incomparable*

2. **subversive** (səb vər´ siv) *adj.* in opposition to authority or
    government
    The king imprisoned the author for writing a book with *subversive* ideas.
    syn: dissident; rebellious   *ant: loyal*

3. **conducive** (kən dōō´ siv) *adj.* tending to cause or bring about
    Job dissatisfaction is often *conducive* to high levels of stress.
    syn: contributive

4. **amenable** (ə mē´ nə bəl) *adj.* agreeable; responsive to suggestion or advice
    The *amenable* boss listened to and acted upon the workers' complaints.
    syn: responsive; tractable   *ant: inflexible*

5. **stricture** (strik´ chər) *n.* a restraint or limit
    Faced with overpopulation, the government enacted harsh *strictures* on
    immigration.
    syn: constraints; limitations

6. **sedentary** (se´ dən ter ē) *adj.* characterized by or requiring sitting;
    motionless
    The regional salesman sought a *sedentary* job that did not require driving
    or heavy lifting every day.
    syn: inactive

7. **influx** (in´ fluks) *n.* an inward flow
    Thanks to wise investing, Meg's bank account had a steady *influx* of money.
                                           ant: outflow

8. **rigorous** (ri´ gə rəs) *adj.* severe; relentless; harsh
    Few people completed the *rigorous* trek to the summit of Mount Everest.
    syn: arduous; grueling   *ant: easy; painless*

9. **patina** (pə tē´ nə) *n.* a sheen on a surface resulting from age and use
    The *patina* on the antique lamp gave the item character but reduced its value.

10. **placebo** (plä sē´ bō) *n.* a fake drug used in the testing of medication
    Half of the test subjects ingested the real drug, and the other half took *placebos*.

11. **junta** (hun´ tə) *n.* a military group ruling a country after seizing power
    After the revolution, a *junta* governed the island nation until elections were held.

12. **pinnacle** (pi´ ni kəl) *n.* a peak or climax
    The *pinnacle* of her career was her two-month trip to Russia.
    syn: summit; apex   *ant: nadir*

13. **mollify** (mä´ lə fī) *v.* to reduce, soothe, or calm
    Amber attempted to *mollify* the baby by singing her a song.
    syn: placate; pacify   *ant: enrage*

14. **perjury** (pər´ jə rē) *n.* the act of lying under oath
    A *perjury* charge added to the length of the guilty man's incarceration.

15. **plaintive** (plān´ tiv) *adj.* expressing sorrow; mournful
    The *plaintive* poem brought tears to her eyes.
    syn: melancholic   *ant: joyful*

Exercise I

Words in Context

From the list below, supply the words needed to complete the paragraph. Some words will not be used.

influx	pinnacle	sedentary	junta
conducive	rigorous	strictures	

1. Heather knew that she would need to impose some _____ on her eating habits in order to comply with her _____ training regimen in the weeks before the marathon. Timing was crucial; in order to place well, Heather would need to reach the _____ of her fitness on the day of the race. Several days of rest before the race will be _____ to her winning, but until that time, no one will be able to regard Heather as _____; if she's not sleeping, she will be running.

From the list below, supply the words needed to complete the paragraph. Some words will not be used.

    perjury   **rigorous**   **influx**   **plaintive**
      amenable   **tantamount**   **mollify**

2. The steady _____ of observers continued until every seat in the courtroom was filled. Everyone watched the famous defendant, who appeared to be _____ to every suggestion from her lawyer as she nodded in affirmation to each whisper from him. While on the stand, the defendant had a[n] _____ look as she described the guilt that she felt for her crimes; however, during the cross-examination, the prosecutor succeeded in provoking the defendant until she lost her temper. She stood and screamed in rage.

   "Defense, please _____ your client," said the judge. After the outburst, the trial fell apart for the defense. The jury deliberated and found the defendant guilty, and one of the witnesses faced _____ charges for lying on behalf of the defendant.

From the list below, supply the words needed to complete the paragraph. Some words will not be used.

    junta   **sedentary**   **mollify**   **subversive**
      patina   **placebo**   **tantamount**

3. The dull _____ on the brass buttons of General Blanco's otherwise perfect uniform was the only outward hint of his inner turmoil. He stepped outside of the capital office and fished in his pockets for his pill box. Only his doctor knew that the general was about to take a[n] _____ that consisted of little more than sugar. Days before, the general had demanded treatment for recurring chest pains. The doctor found nothing wrong with the general, so he prescribed a psychological treatment for what he thought was a psychological illness.

   General Blanco's malady was likely the result of a very stressful situation. At the time the pains began, he was a member of a five-person _____ that had seized control of an impoverished nation, and plenty of _____ citizens would have liked nothing more than to eliminate the militant rulers and reinstall the exiled dictator. Blanco had had some experience _____ to leading his nation, but little experience in dodging assassins.

Exercise II

Sentence Completion

Complete the sentence in a way that shows you understand the meaning of the italicized vocabulary word.

1. Judging by the *patina* on the doorknob, the house...

2. The *junta* took control of the government after...

3. To some employers, taking office supplies for home use is *tantamount* to...

4. The little girl seemed *plaintive* after...

5. During his life, the composer worked in obscurity, but he rose to the pinnacle of his occupation only...

6. The builder said that warm, damp conditions in the basement are *conducive* to...

7. *Strictures* on the number of fish you can catch are meant to...

8. Pauline's *rigorous* morning workout includes...

9. Ted was fired for *perjury* after he...

10. Some *subversive* citizens refused to acknowledge the new law that...

11. Will attributed his fast recovery to the *influx* of ...

12. The photographer required his subjects to be *sedentary* so that...

13. Half of the experimental rats received a *placebo*, while the other half received...

14. The usually *amenable* students in the class surprised the substitute teacher by...

15. The police could not *mollify* the man after he learned that...

Exercise III

Roots, Prefixes, and Suffixes

Study the entries and answer the questions that follow.

The root *phon* means "sound."
The prefix *tele* means "afar" or "at a distance."
The root *put* means "to clean," "to prune," or "to reckon."

1. *Using literal translations as guidance, define the following words without using a dictionary.*

   A. telephone   D. television
   B. repute   E. compute
   C. polyphony   F. symphonic

2. A battlefield surgeon might want to _____ someone's infected limb, but someone who does not think that the operation is necessary might _____ the doctor's decision.

3. List as many words as you can think of that contain the roots *phon* or *put*.

Exercise IV

Inference

Complete the sentences by inferring information about the italicized word from its context.

1. If someone is as *sedentary* as a statue, then that person is…

2. A store might choose an *amenable* person to work in the complaint department because he or she will…

3. If inhalation of asbestos is *conducive* to developing lung cancer, people who work in asbestos mines should…

Exercise V

Writing

Here is a writing prompt similar to the one you will find on the essay writing portion of the ACT.

Public shaming was once a common element of American society, at least in colonial America, before the existence of a complex and universal system of law. Small communities justified public shaming because the population was small and individuals were very dependent on one another—one person's crime, neglect, or oversight could jeopardize the survival of an entire village.

Public shaming is still very much alive in some arguably undeveloped nations and even some industrial nations, but why? Is public shaming an effective form of punishment, or is it merely an opportunity for spectators to feel smug?

In the modern age, relatively minor offenses persist on an individual's record for the rest of his or her life. Would corporal punishment or public shaming be worth the humiliation if it meant that the crime were expunged from one's record upon completion of the punishment, living on only in the memory of the witnesses? Is there a model of this type of (nonviolent) justice that could, or should, be employed in public schools?

Argue your case in a letter to the editor of a large newspaper. Support your arguments with observations and examples that you've read about, experienced, or witnessed for yourself.

Thesis: Write a one-sentence response to the assignment. Make certain this single sentence offers a clear statement of your position.

Example: Most nations have left public shaming in the past because it is a cruel punishment that does not fit with modern civilization.

_____

_____

Organizational Plan: List at least three subtopics you will use to support your main idea. This list is your outline.

1. _____

2. _____

3. _____

Draft: Following your outline, write a good first draft of your essay. Remember to support all your points with examples, facts, references to reading, etc.

Review and Revise: Exchange essays with a classmate. Using the Holistic scoring guide on page 221, score your partner's essay (while he or she scores yours). Focus on the development of ideas and use of language conventions. If necessary, rewrite your essay to correct the problems indicated by the essay's score.

Exercise VI

English Practice

Improving Paragraphs

Read the following passage and then choose the best revision for the underlined portions of the paragraph. The questions will require you to make decisions regarding the revision of the reading selection. Some revisions are not of actual mistakes, but will improve the clarity of the writing.

(1) Clothes hangers are one of mankind's greatest peeves because they are <u>unnecessary</u>[1] evil. (2) The way in which the simple creatures complicate daily life reveals their satanic inclination. (3) Wire hangers are the <u>worst, it is</u>[2] rumored that they exist solely to irritate the user. (4) At night, while humans sleep, wire hangers converse about how they can collectively infuriate people who try to remove hangers from their natural state—the puzzle-like entanglement. (5) Inseparable, the hangers devise ways to best fuse themselves to one another by interweaving their long, <u>thin, arms</u>[3] and necks.

1. A. NO CHANGE
   B. an necessity
   C. a necessary
   D. unnecessarily

2. F. NO CHANGE
   G. worst it is
   H. worst; its
   J. worst; it is

3. A. NO CHANGE
   B. thin arms
   C. thin, arms,
   D. thin arms,

(6) Sadly, humans appear to be years away from solving the coat hanger dilemma. (7) Even in this age of space exploration, digital information, and <u>learning quantum physics</u>,[4] we can find no better way to hang clothing <u>then</u>[5] with hangers. (8) We try hooks, which work fairly well, but they leave permanent divots in garments in the spot on which the garment was hanged. (9) A garment hung by the sleeve, for example, <u>look</u>[6] rather strange when worn with a pointy bulge emanating from the shoulder.

4. F. NO CHANGE
   G. quantum physics,
   H. knowing quantum physics,
   J. learning physics,

5. A. NO CHANGE
   B. accept
   C. than
   D. but

6. F. NO CHANGE
   G. looked
   H. looking
   J. looks

7. Which of the following corrects a usage error in sentence 8?
   A. Hyphenate *fairly well.*
   B. Change *hanged* to *hung.*
   C. Change *permanent* to *temporary.*
   D. Insert a semicolon after *hooks.*

(10) Wood hangers prove only to be greater foes than their wire cousins. (11) They are weighty and bulky, and when they're not used to hang heavy overcoats, they usurp all available space in the closet. (12) When wood hangers are not taking up precious space, they are trying to escape; <u>they're most common</u>[8] method is to grab any adjacent wire hanger as it is picked from the rack. (13) Plastic hangers, while mildly friendlier than wooden hangers, have their own annoying idiosyncrasies, the first being the tiny hook-like appendages that are allegedly for securing the hanging loops of skirts. (14) These little hooks were obviously engineered by clothing manufacturers because they invariably break off and leave sharp edges to fray the inside of the <u>blouse that accompanies</u>[9] the skirt. (15) It's cruel, indeed, but to make things worse, skirts actually hung by their loops develop distinct creases that make re-ironing necessary. (16) Re-ironing is the ultimate goal of any hanger separated from its nest.

8. F. NO CHANGE
   G. their commonest
   H. there most common
   J. their most common

9. A. NO CHANGE
   B. blouse; that accompanies
   C. blouse, which accompanies
   D. blouse, which, accompanying

10. Which of the following would best improve paragraph 3?
    F. Begin a new paragraph after sentence 11.
    G. Begin a new paragraph after sentence 12.
    H. Begin a new paragraph after sentence 13.
    J. Begin a new paragraph after sentence 14.

(17) One particularly devilish species of hanger is the one with the white cardboard roll-on[11] the bottom for hanging slacks without producing a fold mark. (18) These hangers, while not quite as cunning as plastic hangers, are perhaps the most treacherous because they don't even try to function as they are designed. (19) Immediately after placing a load upon the hanger, however minuscule, the cardboard tube collapses into its natural equilibrium—the classic V-shape. (20) The more astute cardboard-roll hangers wait until they have been placed in the closet, out of view, before they collapse. (21) This ensures that they carry out that prime directive of all hangers—to render the clothing wrinkled and unfit for wearing in public.

11. A. NO CHANGE
    B. cardboard roll on
    C. cardboard rollon
    D. cardboard roll, on

(22) No one knows what the future holds for the human-hanger dilemma, but certainly scientists are working around the clock to remedy the blight. (23) Until that solution <u>arrives; we must</u>[12] stay one step ahead of the hangers. (24) We must retaliate and deny their happiness. (25) Ridicule the hanger, and then show it that you're in charge by simply throwing the clothes on the floor and wrinkling them yourself. (26) The next time that you are about to detangle a hanger, stop.

12. F. NO CHANGE
    G. arrives—we must
    H. arrive we must
    J. arrives, we must

13. Which of the following suggestions would improve the introduction of the passage?
    A. Start a new paragraph with sentence 5.
    B. Start paragraph 1 with sentence 6.
    C. Start a new paragraph after sentence 2.
    D. Start a new paragraph after sentence 3.

14. Which change to the paragraph sequence would improve the organization of the passage?
    F. Exchange paragraph 1 with paragraph 3.
    G. Exchange paragraph 2 with paragraph 3.
    H. Move paragraph 2 so it follows paragraph 4.
    J. Delete paragraph 2.

15. Which of the following best clarifies paragraph 5?
    A. Exchange sentence 22 with sentence 23.
    B. Exchange sentence 25 with sentence 26.
    C. Exchange sentence 24 with sentence 25.
    D. Delete sentence 26.

Vocabulary
Power Plus
for the
ACT
Vocabulary,
Reading, and Writing
Exercises for High Scores

Lesson Twenty

1. **impasse** (im´ pas) *n.* a problem or predicament with no obvious resolution
    Fighting resumed when the two factions reached an *impasse* during the peace talks.
    syn: gridlock; stalemate; standoff

2. **wunderkind** (vun´ dər kint) *n.* one who excels in a difficult field at an early age
    The ten-year-old *wunderkind* mastered organic chemistry while his peers learned the basics of long division.
    syn: prodigy

3. **acumen** (ə kyü´ mən) *n.* ability to discern or discriminate; shrewdness
    Hal's business *acumen* made him an excellent stock broker.
    syn: keenness; sharpness   *ant: ignorance; naiveté*

4. **nanotechnology** (na nō tek nä´ lə jē) *n.* the use of single atoms and molecules to construct microscopic devices
    Scientists hope to use *nanotechnology* to create tiny robots that can be injected into the body to destroy cancer cells.

5. **notarize** (nō´ tə rīz) *v.* to certify legally
    Someone will *notarize* the signatures on the title to complete the sale of a car.

6. **piquant** (pē´ känt) *adj.* a strong, stimulating taste
    A mix of herbs and spices gave Joe's chili a *piquant* taste.
    syn: spicy; tangy   *ant: bland*

7. **malodorous** (mal ō´ də rəs) *adj.* having an offensive odor
    People ten miles away could smell the *malodorous* chicken processing plant.
    syn: stinking

8. **pungent** (pən´ jənt) *adj.* a sharp taste or smell; acrid
    The dairy store offered samples of both mild and *pungent* types of cheeses.
    syn: sharp   *ant: mild*

9. **erroneous** (i rō′ nē əs) *adj.* incorrect; mistaken
    Read the questions carefully, or you'll have *erroneous* answers on the test.
    syn: flawed   *ant: correct*

10. **concurrent** (kən kər′ ənt) *adj.* happening at the same time
    This year, Jane's birthday happens to be *concurrent* with Easter.
    syn: simultaneous   *ant: conflicting; separate*

11. **negligible** (ne′ gli jə bəl) *adj.* of little importance; insignificant
    The car was in great shape except for a few *negligible* scratches.
    syn: unimportant; trifling   *ant: significant; noteworthy*

12. **renege** (ri nig′) *v.* to break a promise or obligation; revoke
    Pete *reneged* on his promise to care for his dog, so his parents gave the
    animal away.
    syn: breach; abandon

13. **precept** (prē′ sept) *n.* a rule of action; a principle to live by
    Kim lived by the *precepts* of modesty, courtesy, and moderation.
    syn: law; axiom; belief

14. **visage** (vi′ zij) *n.* a face or facial expression
    Ken's *visage* turned to anger when he saw the neighbor's dog in his own
    swimming pool.
    syn: countenance; features

15. **irrevocable** (i re′ və kə bəl) *adj.* impossible to retract or revoke;
      irreversible
    The decision to divorce was *irrevocable.*

    syn: permanent; unchangeable

Exercise I

Words in Context

From the list below, supply the words needed to complete the paragraph. Some words will not be used.

renege	precept	pungent	notarize
negligible	acumen	visage	erroneous

1. Dave could not help noticing Daria's furious _____ as she pulled her sputtering car into his driveway. She parked the car and stomped across the lawn until she found Dave sitting on the porch.

    "I want my money back," said Daria. "I've had the car for only an hour, so it shouldn't be a problem for you to return the money. This whole episode has left a[n] _____, ugly taste in my mouth."

    "I'm afraid that your assumption is _____," said Dave in a smug tone. "The clerk _____ the sales contract; you bought the car 'as-is,' and the transaction is official. You can't _____ on the deal at this point. Besides, it's not my fault that you didn't have the _____ to realize that the car is not what you wanted." Daria made fists, grumbled, and stormed back to the lemon that she had just purchased.

From the list below, supply the words needed to complete the paragraph. Some words will not be used.

nanotechnology	precept	pungent	wunderkind
irrevocable	impasse	concurrent	

2. "Every word is recorded in this laboratory, so use caution because anything you say will be considered _____," Dr. Bryant warned Matt as they walked past the _____ department of the robotics research division. Matt was still ecstatic about his new job with Neutrodyne, a world leader in robotic technology. Like many of the research staff, Matt had been a[n] _____ who had completed high school and college by the age of seventeen. Now, at twenty-six, he had a doctorate in physics and was the first choice for recruiters from several major corporations, three of which were government contractors. Matt had decided to take the job with Neutrodyne because he was afraid that he might reach a[n] _____ working for the government if his political views did not support the nature of his assigned research. He wanted the ability to merge his _____ with his career, and Neutrodyne seemed to be the best place to do it.

From the list below, supply the words needed to complete the paragraph. Some words will not be used.

malodorous	negligible	impasse	piquant
concurrent	acumen		

3. Since the Soup Olympics and the Champion Cookoff were _____ this year, Kevin had to make two separate batches of his famous seafood bisque. He stayed up all night before the contests, stirring and adding tiny amounts of _____ spices until he felt that the soup was perfect. To an inexperienced taster, Kevin's tiny additions produced _____ changes in the food, but to the judges, Kevin knew, the tiny differences would determine who won and who lost. If the bisque lacked in one particular spice, or if the judge detected the faintest _____ scent from the sample, Kevin would forfeit first prize.

Exercise II

Sentence Completion

Complete the sentence in a way that shows you understand the meaning of the italicized vocabulary word.

1. If Dianne had known that her decision was going to be *irrevocable*, she...

2. Since the flood was *concurrent* with the earthquake, the damage...

3. If no one *notarizes* the contract, it will...

4. After fleeing the police, the mugger found himself at an *impasse* when he...

5. Norman's youthful *visage* disappeared after...

6. The back parking lot was *malodorous* in the summer because...

7. At only six years of age, the *wunderkind* could...

8. Brad's parents were confident that their son had the *precepts* to...

9. To give the bread a *pungent* flavor, the cook...

10. The expert in *nanotechnology* lectured the students on...

11. Paul *reneged* on his dinner plans when he found out...

12. One *erroneous* entry in the database will cause...

13. Lovers of *piquant* food came from miles around to try...

14. Rhonda told the pizza-delivery man to keep the *negligible* amount of...

15. Teri's *acumen* in identifying personality types made her good at...

Exercise III

Roots, Prefixes, and Suffixes

Study the entries and answer the questions that follow.

The prefixes *ambi* and *amphi* mean "both" or "around."
The roots *luc* and *lum* mean "light."
The prefix *super* means "above" or "over."
The root *magn* means "great."

1. *Using literal translations as guidance, define the following words without using a dictionary.*

    A. luminary   D. magnitude
    B. translucent   E. magnate
    C. amphibious   F. superintendent

2. Someone who can use both hands equally well is called _____. An *ambiguous* statement can be interpreted in _____.

3. You might use a lamp to _____ your desktop so that you can see your work. If the filament in the light bulb does not become _____, you will know that the bulb is burned out.

4. List as many words as you can think of that contain the root *magn* or the prefix *super*.

Exercise IV

Inference

Complete the sentences by inferring information about the italicized word from its context.

1. If you *renege* on a deal once, few people will...

2. Sports stars and team owners might reach an *impasse* about contracts if...

3. One good *precept* to remember throughout your life is...

Exercise V

Critical Reading

Below is a reading passage followed by several multiple-choice questions similar to the ones you will encounter on the ACT. Carefully read the passage and choose the best answer for each of the questions.

Lots of people celebrate Halloween, but only a few realize that the origins of the autumn celebration rest in ancient history. The predominant theory about the origins of Halloween is that the celebration descended from the ancient Celtic festival of Samhain.

5   For the Celts living in Ireland and northern England during the fifth century B.C., Samhain was the most important festival of the year. Celebrated on the first of November, Samhain honored the end of the year and marked the beginning of the new year. For the Celts, November was a logical time to observe the new year; November marked the end of the harvest season, and it heralded the onset of

10   winter, a potentially deadly season for early cultures. It was only appropriate that the unstoppable winter, whose biting cold and long dark nights drained the life from both crops and people, was a symbol of death. On the eve of the Celtic New Year—the night that we now call Halloween—the Celts believed that a doorway to the spirit world opened, and that the spirits of those who died throughout the year

15   were free to once again roam the world of the living. During the eve of the new year, the Celts wore costumes, while priests conducted rituals around sacrificial pyres.

The beliefs and traditions associated with Samhain slowly changed in the centuries following the peak of Celtic civilization. Romans conquered most of the Celtic lands and had incorporated some of their own beliefs into the Samhain

20   festivities by A.D. 100. After Christianity had spread to Celtic lands by the eighth century, the day of the Celtic New Year became All-hallows, a day of honoring Christian saints. We now refer to the eve of November first as All-hallows Eve, or Halloween; despite cultural shifts, however, the descendents of the Celts never quite abandoned the ancient belief that spirits roamed the earth on Halloween. People

25   augmented the old Celtic beliefs with new legends, the most notable of which was perhaps the legend that spirits not only roamed the earth, but that they also sought new bodies to possess.

Wary of spirit possession, the Celtic descendents had to develop adequate defenses, the first of which was disguise. Having assumed that spirits would ignore

30   their own kind, people disguised themselves as spirits if they ventured outdoors on Halloween. As a second precaution, people placed offerings of food on their doorsteps; they hoped that any evil spirits roaming the night would be satisfied with the food and decline to enter the homes. People who left no treat for the spirits, of course, risked provoking the wandering spirits and rendering themselves prone to

35   the devices of vindictive spirits.

The Halloween that America knows did not come into practice until the late nineteenth century. Long dormant in America, the celebration experienced a resurgence when the influx of Irish and Scottish immigrants brought old Celtic traditions to North America. Americans began dressing up in costumes and, in
40 merriment, went from house to house asking for food. People who offered no food were subject to tricks—good-humored "punishments" for their lack of hospitality.

As poverty increased around the twentieth century, young urbanites began to taint the benevolent spirit of Halloween. What were once benign tricks slowly became acts of vandalism that only detracted from the autumn festivities. Fearing
45 that such behavior might destroy an enjoyable tradition, people planned ways to turn Halloween into a community event.

Shortly after the turn of the century, communities organized block parties, dances, and other Halloween festivities that brought people together and, at the same time, discouraged the destructive activities of mischievous pranksters. People
50 were encouraged to offer small treats as a way to rekindle the festive nature of Halloween and to curb vandalism. This was the birth of the still-popular American Halloween tradition.

Few of the modern Halloween revelers stop to think about the historic roots of the holiday. Many people incorrectly assume that the holiday symbolizes an
55 assemblage of evil rituals or devil worship, but that is certainly not the case. While the Celts did perhaps believe that spirits roamed the earth on the eve of the new year, the traditions that they established were innocent and festive, just as they are today. Halloween will always be a source of fun childhood memories and a way to celebrate, or even parody, our fears of the unknown.

1. The original Celts observed Samhain around which of the following time periods?
    A. 1941-1945 B.C.
    B. 400-500 B.C.
    C. A.D. 100-200
    D. A.D. 700-800

2. The ancient Celts celebrated Samhain for the same reason that modern people might celebrate
    F. President's Day.
    G. Halloween.
    H. New Year.
    J. Valentine's Day.

3. According to the passage, winter was an appropriate symbol of death because
    A. it killed food supplies.
    B. it caused people to freeze.
    C. it caused the death of plants and people.
    D. it slowed the movement of the spirits.

4. Descendents of the Celts thought that disguises would protect them from spirits because
    F. the ancient Celts wore costumes and lived through Halloween.
    G. they thought that spirits would not bother other spirits.
    H. they thought that the spirits would not be able to find them.
    J. spirits could not understand the way that Celts looked.

5. In line 25 of the first passage, the word *augmented* most nearly means
    A. supplemented.
    B. rewrote.
    C. abolished.
    D. believed.

6. The intent of the passage is to
    F. persuade that Halloween is not evil.
    G. inform how Halloween influenced the rituals of Samhain.
    H. develop an argument against Halloween.
    J. inform about the early roots of Halloween traditions.

7. According to the passage, modern Halloween tricks were originally
    A. scornful songs that trick-or-treaters sang when they were not satisfied with their treats.
    B. ways for spirits to enter homes.
    C. severe punishments imposed on people who offered no food.
    D. harmless "punishments" played on people who provided no treats.

8. Which choice best describes why Halloween was threatened during the turn of the century?
    F. Poverty increased.
    G. Celtic people abandoned their traditions.
    H. Children had discipline problems.
    J. Vandalism increased during Halloween.

9. As used in line 43, *benign* most nearly means
    A. harmless.
    B. expensive.
    C. legendary.
    D. careless.

10. The most appropriate title for the passages is
    F. America's Favorite Holiday.
    G. Ancient Halloween.
    H. Modern Halloween.
    J. The History of Halloween.

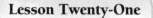

Vocabulary
Power Plus
for the ACT
Vocabulary,
Reading, and Writing
Exercises for High Scores

Lesson Twenty-One

1. **confute** (kən fyōōt´) *v.* to argue or point out error
The candidate *confuted* every aspect of his opponent's proposed policies.
syn: refute; disprove   *ant: confirm; verify*

2. **meritorious** (mer ə tōr´ ē əs) *adj.* deserving of an award or honor
The young corporal won a medal for his *meritorious* actions in combat.
syn: commendable; laudable; praiseworthy   *ant: despicable; unworthy*

3. **mezzanine** (mez ə nēn´) *n.* the lowest balcony in a theater; a partial
story between main stories in a building
Kelly had an excellent view of the show from her seat in the *mezzanine*.

4. **tribulation** (tri byə lā´ shən) *n.* an affliction, trouble, or difficult
experience
The death of Betty's father was a time of *tribulation* for the entire family.
syn: ordeal; hardship

5. **recumbent** (ri kəm´ bənt) *adj.* resting or lying down
The *recumbent* children soon fell asleep.
syn: reclining   *ant: upright*

6. **dynasty** (dī´ nəs tē) *n.* a succession of rulers from the same family or
group
The Romanov *Dynasty* ruled Russia for more than 300 years.

7. **purport** (pər pôrt´) *v.* to claim; to have or to give the false impression
of being
The newspaper *purports* to be objective, but it is actually very biased in its
reporting.
syn: allege; claim; maintain

8. **forte** (fôrt, fôr´ tā) *n.* an area of expertise or strength
Jane is good at mathematics, but science is her *forte*.
syn: specialty; talent   *ant: weakness*

9. **kleptomania** (klep tə mān´ ē ə) *n.* a continual urge to steal regardless
of economic motive
Unable to control her *kleptomania*, the wealthy actress shoplifted a pair of
shoes.

10. **renown**   (ri noun´)   *n.*   state of being well known and honored; fame
The actor enjoyed world *renown* after starring in a blockbuster film.
syn: notoriety; popularity   *ant: anonymity; obscurity*

11. **ineffable**   (i ne´ fə bəl)   *adj.*   too sacred or great to be described;
indescribable
Lynn could not believe the *ineffable* beauty of the mountains in the distance.
syn: inexpressible; unspeakable

12. **fortitude**   (for´ tə tōōd)   *n.*   strength in adversity
If not for the *fortitude* of the soldiers on the front line, we would have lost
the battle.
syn: determination; tenacity   *ant: weakness*

13. **botch**   (bätch)   *v.*   to ruin through clumsiness; to bungle
Bill *botched* the experiment when he forgot to water the plants.
                                                       ant: fix

14. **perennial**   (pə ren´ ē əl)   *adj.*   lasting indefinitely
The parents tried to instill a *perennial* feeling of worth in their child.
syn: enduring; perpetual   *ant: fleeting; limited*

15. **brinkmanship**   (brink´ mən ship)   *n.*   pushing dangerous situations to the
edge of disaster rather than conceding
President Kennedy's blockade during the Cuban Missile Crisis could have
led to nuclear war, but this act of *brinkmanship* ended with the peaceful
removal of weapons.

Exercise I

Words in Context

From the list below, supply the words needed to complete the paragraph. Some words will not be used.

renown	forte	confute	brinkmanship
dynasty	recumbent	tribulation	

1. Damian mounted his new _____ bicycle, but he immediately crashed into a light pole because he was not used to sitting back while riding a bike. After a few minutes of _____, though, he was able to ride around the parking lot without falling. Damian's friends _____ his decision to spend a lot of money on what they called a novelty item, but Damian was _____ for wasting money on things that sat in the basement and collected dust when he tired of them. His credit card sprees would stop eventually. Damian was bound to lose his game of financial _____, in which he waited to pay his bills until he received threatening notices from the bank.

From the list below, supply the words needed to complete the paragraph. Some words will not be used.

fortitude	perennial	recumbent	purport
forte	botch	meritorious	

2. Mohandas Gandhi never _____ himself to be a great leader, and his _____ was certainly not his public speaking ability. Nonetheless, Gandhi's _____ service to his people brought independence to India, and his _____ message, that any nation willing to unite in patience and _____ can overcome its oppressors, will be remembered forever.

From the list below, supply the words needed to complete the paragraph. Some words will not be used.

mezzanine	dynasty	tribulation	kleptomania
botch	meritorious	ineffable	

3. During preparation for his twenty-first burglary, Simon wondered if, perhaps, he suffered from a type of _____. He had already amassed a small fortune from the sale of stolen art, but he always seemed to need to pull off "just one more job" before he retired permanently. He almost retired involuntarily when he _____ the last job by dropping a statuette of _____ beauty from the _____ of the art museum while fumbling with his night vision goggles. The relic, which dated back to the Ming _____, shattered when it struck the floor far below.

Exercise II

Sentence Completion

Complete the sentence in a way that shows you understand the meaning of the italicized vocabulary word.

1. Jake planned to spend his afternoon *recumbent* in...

2. Judy longed for the life of *renown* that only...

3. I *confuted* the question on the test because it...

4. From the *mezzanine* in the factory, the foreman shouted...

5. If math is not your *forte*, then you should...

6. Davy *botched* the car's paint job when he...

7. The hostage crisis turned into a dangerous game of *brinkmanship* when the criminal threatened to...

8. The school honored Nicole's *meritorious* academic achievements by...

9. It is important for citizens to maintain their *fortitude* during...

10. Unless you have some form of *kleptomania*, there's no reason for you...

11. In a few minutes, the *tribulation* of learning how to swim was over and Clarence was able to...

12. For two hundred years, the *dynasty*...

13. The man *purports* to be an expert, but really he...

14. The *ineffable* sight of the Earth from the spacecraft caused...

15. April hoped to find *perennial* happiness by...

Exercise III

Roots, Prefixes, and Suffixes

Study the entries and answer the questions that follow.

The roots *doc* and *doct* mean "to teach" or "to cause."
The roots *au* and *esthe* mean "to feel," "to perceive," or "to hear."
The roots *cad* and *cas* mean "to fall" or "to die."

1. Using literal translations as guidance, define the following words without using a dictionary.

   A. document   D. audition
   B. auditorium   E. anesthetize
   C. cadence   F. aesthetic

2. The word _____ literally translates to "teacher," and a _____ student is easy to teach.

3. A _____ is a dead or fallen soldier, and medical students practice their surgical techniques on *cadavers*, which are _____.

4. List as many words as you can think of that contain the root *au*.

Exercise IV

Inference

Complete the sentences by inferring information about the italicized word from its context.

1. If you continue to *confute* the boss in front of the other workers, you might...

2. For her *meritorious* actions that saved two lives, the lifeguard was...

3. Because he was *recumbent* in his hammock, Pete did not...

Exercise V

Writing

Here is a writing prompt similar to the one you will find on the essay writing portion of the ACT.

It is no secret that many, if not most, behavior problems among students begin with problems at home. Student misconduct is often attributed to parents or guardians who fail to impart manners and mutual respect to their children, which results in children who are socially inept and disruptive to other students.

Some schools are attempting to reach complacent parents and guardians by enacting fines to accompany student misconduct. Students who are caught violating school policies will be ticketed, much like speeders receive tickets from police. Because students will rarely have the funds to pay their own fines, the responsibility will fall on parents. If detention or suspension fails to gain the attention of the parents, it is thought, then, that perhaps an invoice will.

Is fining students for misbehavior a legitimate means of punishment? In deciding your position, consider the actual monetary costs of traditional punishments. Does the school, amid widespread budget cuts, have to pay a teacher overtime to deal with problem students, or repair damage done to school property?

Write a letter to the school board either advocating or contesting a fine policy. Support your argument with at least three subtopics as to why fines should or should not be enacted.

Thesis: Write a one-sentence response to the assignment. Make certain this single sentence offers a clear statement of your position.

Example: Fines for misbehavior would motivate disruptive students to get on the right track.

_____

_____

Organizational Plan: List at least three subtopics you will use to support your main idea. This list is your outline.

1. _____

2. _____

3. _____

Draft: Following your outline, write a good first draft of your essay. Remember to support all your points with examples, facts, references to reading, etc.

Review and Revise: Exchange essays with a classmate. Using the Holistic scoring guide on page 221, score your partner's essay (while her or she scores yours). If necessary, rewrite your essay to correct the problems noted by your partner.

Exercise VI

English Practice

Identifying Sentence Errors
Identify the errors in the following sentences. Choose the answer that fixes the error. If the sentence contains no error, select NO CHANGE.

1. When people buy cell phones, <u>you should</u> be able to afford the roaming charges.
   A. NO CHANGE
   B. it should
   C. they should
   D. they could

2. The psychiatrist found that Marguerite had no <u>self-confidence in herself</u> whatsoever.
   F. NO CHANGE
   G. self-confidence in her
   H. self-confidence of her own
   J. self-confidence

3. We thought <u>it was bazaar</u> to see Marvin wear his toupee backwards, but he seemed to think it was cute.
   A. NO CHANGE
   B. it is bazaar
   C. it was bizarre
   D. it to be bizarre

4. The next time that you go to the office store, I would like you to get me these <u>kind of pens.</u>
   F. NO CHANGE
   G. kinds of pens.
   H. type of pens.
   J. kind of pen's.

5. If Bob had begun the inspection earlier, <u>he would have</u> completed the required repairs before the general's visit.
   A. NO CHANGE
   B. he should have
   C. he will have
   D. he would of

Improving Sentences

The underlined portion of each sentence below contains some flaw. Select the answer that best corrects the flaw.

6. <u>His new pinstriped suit was worn by him</u> to the last dance of the school year.
    A. He wore a pinstriped suit
    B. His pinstriped suit, new, was worn
    C. He wore his new pinstriped suit
    D. His worn pinstriped suit he wore

7. Pat based the decision for his testimony on the old <u>proverb that honesty was the best policy.</u>
    F. proverb: that honesty was the best policy.
    G. proverb "that honesty is the best policy."
    H. proverb that honesty is the best policy.
    J. proverb: "Honesty is the best policy."

8. Teachers have shown that children have a keener aptitude <u>for learning than an adult.</u>
    A. for learning than adults have.
    B. for adult-level learning.
    C. than an adult has for learning.
    D. for learning than adults.

9. <u>We had an upright piano built for a student with a transparent front.</u>
    F. We had an upright piano built with a transparent front for a student.
    G. We had an upright piano with a transparent front built for a student.
    H. We had a student upright piano with transparent front built.
    J. We had a transparent front upright piano that was built for a student.

10. <u>Don't expect Harold, Mimi, and I</u> to arrive promptly at an early morning meeting.
    A. Don't expect Harold, Mimi, and me
    B. Harold, Mimi, and me should not be expected
    C. Harold, Mimi and I cannot be expected
    D. Don't expect Mimi, I, and Harold

Vocabulary
Power Plus
for the **ACT** Vocabulary, Reading, and Writing Exercises for High Scores

REVIEW
Lessons 15–21

Exercise I

Sentence Completion

Choose the best pair of words to complete the sentence. Most choices will fit grammatically and will even make sense logically, but you must choose the pair that best fits the idea of the sentence.

1. At the _____ of his decline, the former chief executive, penniless, spent a few weeks as a(n) _____, looking for handouts on the street.
   A. junta, pariah
   B. nadir, mendicant
   C. visage, placebo
   D. renown, fiat
   E. acumen, wunderkind

2. Robbie liked the new nature trail, but he feared that the _____ of tourists would _____ the natural beauty of the old forest.
   A. influx, desecrate
   B. impasse, delete
   C. forte, belabor
   D. hilarity, oust
   E. penchant, renege

3. The county judge quickly _____ the sheriff who was convicted of _____ during a murder trial.
   A. notarized, fidelity
   B. daubed, brinkmanship
   C. admonished, chicanery
   D. mitigated, tribulation
   E. ousted, perjury

4. When the _____ became too corrupt and ineffective, a(n) _____ element of the king's court developed a plan to replace the ruling family.
    A. dynasty, subversive
    B. kleptomania, zaftig
    C. manifesto, ineffable
    D. genealogy, faux
    E. impasse, meritorious

5. The city hired _____ police officers to keep the peace among _____ fans leaving the stadium.
    A. perennial, quintessential
    B. adjunct, rambunctious
    C. palpable, concurrent
    D. fluent, recumbent
    E. macabre, monolithic

6. Having been left with only ten percent leg function after the disease, Rena engaged in a(n) _____ regimen of physical therapy to overcome her _____.
    A. aloof, tribulation
    B. impermeable, foray
    C. rigorous, affliction
    D. feisty, placebo
    E. irrevocable, nadir

7. In economic terms, the _____ skyscraper made any interest in renting the nearby, shorter buildings, almost _____ by comparison.
    A. monolithic, negligible
    B. piquant, faux
    C. recumbent, imperturbable
    D. impervious, plaintive
    E. concurrent, lax

8. As a way to _____ the damage from the flooding river, the villagers quickly constructed a(n) _____ levee out of sandbags and boulders.
    A. renege, impermeable
    B. deplete, materialistic
    C. oscillate, sedentary
    D. botch, palpable
    E. mitigate, rudimentary

Exercise II

Crossword Puzzle

Use the clues to complete the crossword puzzle. The answers consist of vocabulary words from lessons 15 through 21.

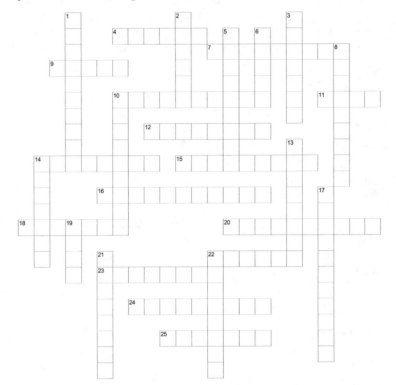

Across

4. ability to discern; shrewdness
7. schoolteacher
9. reserved; distant
10. in opposition to authority
11. prejudiced view; a preference
12. to make less severe
14. peak or climax
15. strength in adversity
16. basic; not refined
18. to argue or point out error
20. of little importance; insignificant
22. social outcast
23. to distribute or allot
24. tending to cause or bring about
25. problem with no obvious resolution

Down

1. anything causing great suffering
2. to break a promise
3. offspring; children
5. beggar
6. a concealed store of goods
8. ambiguous; intentionally vague
10. restraint or limit
13. to warn; to caution in counsel
14. to claim
17. difficult experience
19. artificial
21. absurd; ridiculously clumsy
22. strong liking

Scoring Guide for the ACT Writing Test

ORGANIZATION

6 = Clearly Competent

The paper is clearly organized around the central point or main idea. The organization may grow from the writer's argument or a slightly predictable structure. Ideas follow a logical order.

The work is **free of surface errors** (grammar, spelling, punctuation, etc.).

5 = Reasonably Competent

The organization of the paper is clear, but not fully implemented. The structure might be predictable. Ideas follow a logical order, but transitions might be simple or obvious.

Minor surface errors are present, but they **do not interfere** with the reader's understanding of the work.

4 = Adequately Competent

The organization of the paper is apparent, but not consistently implemented. The structure is predictable. Some ideas follow a logical order, but transitions are simple and obvious.

Surface errors are present, but they **do not severely interfere** with the reader's understanding.

3 = Nearly Competent

There is evidence of a simple organizational plan. Ideas are grouped logically in parts of the paper, but do not flow logically throughout. Transitions are needed.

Surface errors are **apparent** and **begin to interfere** with the reader's understanding of the work.

2 = Marginally Incompetent

The organizational plan of the paper is obscured by too few details and/or irrelevant details. Some of the ideas are grouped logically in parts of the paper. Transitions are needed or are incorrect.

Surface errors are **frequent and severe enough** to **interfere** with the reader's understanding of the work.

1 = Incompetent

There is no clear organizational plan and/or insufficient material. Ideas are not grouped logically. Transitions are absent.

Surface errors are **frequent** and **extreme,** and **severely interfere** with the reader's understanding of the work.

Scoring Guide for the ACT Writing Test

DEVELOPMENT

6 = Clearly Competent

The **paper takes a position** on the issue and **offers sufficient material** (details, examples, anecdotes, supporting facts, etc.) to create a **complete discussion. Every word and sentence is relevant.** Ideas are **fully supported.** The paper visits **different perspectives** of the argument or addresses **counterarguments** to the writer's position. The paper **focuses** on the argument evoked by the prompt. There is a **clear, purposed,** well developed **introduction** and **conclusion.**

The work is **free of surface errors** (grammar, spelling, punctuation, etc.).

5 = Reasonably Competent

The essay **takes a position** on the issue and **offers sufficient material** for a complete discussion, but the reader is left **with a few unanswered questions.**

Ideas are **supported.** The paper **partially visits different perspectives** of the argument or addresses **counterarguments. Most** of the paper **focuses** on the argument evoked by the prompt. There is **no irrelevant material.** There is a clear **introduction** and **conclusion.**

Minor surface errors are present, but they **do not interfere** with the reader's understanding of the work.

4 = Adequately Competent

The paper **takes a position** on the issue but **does not provide** enough details, examples, or supporting facts for a complete discussion, leaving a **few unanswered questions.** The paper includes **some attention** to **counterarguments** and differing perspectives. **Irrelevant material** is present. **Most** of the paper **focuses** on the topic and the specific argument. **Surface errors** are present, but they **do not severely interfere** with the reader's understanding.

3 = Nearly Competent

The essay **takes a position** on the issue but **does not include** sufficient details, examples, or supporting facts for a discussion. The paper **may include incomplete or unclear counterarguments.** The paper **might repeat** details or rhetoric. The paper focuses on the topic, but **does not maintain** the specific argument.

Surface errors are **apparent** and **begin to interfere** with the reader's understanding of the work.

2 = Marginally Incompetent

The paper **may not take a position** on the issue, or the paper may take a position but **fail to support** it with sufficient details. Examples and ideas are **vague** and **irrelevant**. The paper might **repeat ideas extensively**. The paper **might maintain focus** on the general topic.

Surface errors are **frequent and severe enough** to **interfere** with the reader's understanding of the work.

1 = Incompetent

The paper **might attempt to take a position**, but it **fails to provide** examples, fact, or rhetoric to support the position. The paper may be **repetitious** with **little** or **no focus** on the general topic.

Surface errors are **frequent** and **extreme**, and **severely interfere** with the reader's understanding of the work.

Scoring Guide for the ACT Writing Test

SENTENCE FORMATION AND VARIETY

6 = Clearly Competent

Sentences are **varied, complete,** and **assist the reader** in the flow of the discussion.

The work is **free of surface errors** (grammar, spelling, punctuation, etc.).

5 = Reasonably Competent

Sentences are **somewhat varied, generally correct,** and **do not distract** the reader from the flow of the discussion.

Minor surface errors are present, but they **do not interfere** with the reader's understanding of the work.

4 = Adequately Competent

Some sentences show **variety,** and **most** are **complete** and **generally correct.**

Surface errors are present, but they **do not interfere** with the reader's understanding.

3 = Nearly Competent

Sentences show a **little variety,** but the structure may be **dull.** Sentences are **generally complete** and grammatically correct, but **some errors** distract the reader.

Surface errors are **apparent** and **begin to interfere** with the reader's understanding of the work.

2 = Marginally Incompetent

Sentence Structure is usually simple. Problems in sentence structure and grammar distract the reader and provide little or no variety.

Surface errors are **frequent and severe enough** to **interfere** with the reader's understanding of the work.

1 = Incompetent

Sentence structure is **simple, generally erroneous** and **lacks variety.**

Surface errors are **frequent** and **extreme,** and **severely interfere** with the reader's understanding of the work.

Scoring Guide for the ACT Writing Test

WORD CHOICE

6 = Clearly Competent

The essay shows a **good command** of language. Word choice is **specific**, **clear**, and **vivid**, favoring **powerful nouns** and **verbs** to weaker adjective and adverb phrases. **Clear, specific words** are used, instead of vague, general terms.

The work is **free of surface errors** (grammar, spelling, punctuation, etc.).

5 = Reasonably Competent

Language is **competent**. Word choice is **clear** and **accurate**. Words and phrases are **mostly** vivid, specific, and powerful.

Minor surface errors are present, but they **do not interfere** with the reader's understanding of the work.

4 = Adequately Competent

Language is **adequate**, with **appropriate** word choice. **Most** words and phrases are vivid, specific, and powerful.

Serious surface errors are present, but they **do not interfere** with the reader's understanding.

3 = Nearly Competent

Language shows a **basic control** and word choice is **usually appropriate** but **inconsistent**.

Surface errors are **apparent** and **begin to interfere** with the reader's understanding of the work.

2 = Marginally Incompetent

Word choice is usually **vague**.

Surface errors are **frequent** and **severe enough** to **interfere** with the reader's understanding of the work.

1 = Incompetent

Word choice is **simple, vague**, and **inexact**. The writer makes **no attempt** to choose the best words for the topic, audience, and purpose.

Surface errors are **frequent** and **extreme**, and **severely interfere** with the reader's understanding of the work.

Scoring Guide for the ACT Writing Test

HOLISTIC

6 = Clearly Competent

The paper is **clearly organized** around the central idea. Ideas follow a **logical order**.

The paper **takes a position** on the issue and **offers sufficient material** (details, examples, anecdotes, supporting facts, etc.) to create a complete discussion. There is a **clear**, **purposed**, **well developed** introduction and conclusion.

The paper visits **different perspectives** of the argument or addresses **counterarguments** to the writer's position.

Sentences are **varied**, **complete**, and **assist the reader** in the flow of the discussion.

The paper shows a **good command** of language. Word choice is **specific**, **clear**, and **vivid**, favoring **powerful nouns** and **verbs** to weaker adjective and adverb phrases.

The work is **free of surface errors** (grammar, spelling, punctuation, etc.).

5 = Reasonably Competent

The organization of the paper is **clear**, but **not fully implemented**. Ideas follow a **logical order**, but transitions **might be simple** or obvious. The structure **might be predictable**.

The paper **takes a position** on the issue and **offers sufficient material** for a complete discussion, but the reader is left with **a few unanswered questions**. There is a clear **introduction** and **conclusion**.

The paper visits **some different perspectives** of the argument or addresses **counterarguments**.

Sentences are **somewhat varied**, **generally correct**, and **do not distract** the reader from the flow of the discussion.

Language is **competent**. Words and phrases are **mostly vivid, specific**, and **powerful**.

Minor surface errors are present, but they **do not interfere** with the reader's understanding of the work.

4 = Adequately Competent

The organization of the paper is **apparent**, but **not consistently** implemented. The structure is **predictable**. **Some** ideas follow a **logical order**, but transitions are **simple** and **obvious**. **Most** of the paper **focuses** on the topic and the specific argument.

The paper **takes a position** on the issue, but **does not provide** the details, examples, or supporting facts for a complete discussion, leaving **a few unanswered questions**.

The paper includes **little attention** to counterarguments and differing perspectives.

Irrelevant material is present.

Language is **adequate**, with appropriate word choice. **Most** words and phrases are vivid, specific, and powerful.

Some sentences show **variety**, and **most** are **complete** and **generally correct**.

Surface errors are present, but they **do not interfere** with the reader's understanding.

3 = Nearly Competent

There is **evidence of a simple organizational plan**. The essay **takes a position** on the issue but **does not include** sufficient details, examples, or supporting facts for a discussion. Ideas are **grouped logically** in parts of the paper, **but do not flow** logically throughout. The paper **focuses** on the topic, but **does not maintain** the specific argument.

The paper **may include incomplete** or **unclear** counterarguments.

Language shows a **basic control**, and word choice is **usually appropriate** but **inconsistent**. Sentences show a **little variety**, but the structure may be **dull**.

Sentences are **generally complete** and **grammatically correct**, but some errors **distract** the reader.

The paper might **repeat** details or rhetoric.

Surface errors are **apparent** and **begin to interfere** with the reader's understanding of the work.

2 = Marginally Incompetent

The organizational plan of the paper is **obscured by too few details** and/or **irrelevant details**. The paper **may not take a position** on the issue, or the paper may take a position but **fail to support** it with sufficient details. **Some** of the ideas are **grouped logically** in parts of the paper. The paper **generally maintains focus** on the general topic.

Examples and ideas are **vague** and **irrelevant**.

Sentence structure is **usually simple**. **Problems** in sentence structure and grammar **distract** the reader and provide **little** or **no variety**. **Word choice** is usually **vague**.

The paper might **repeat** ideas **extensively**.

Surface errors are **frequent and severe enough** to **interfere** with the reader's understanding of the work.

1 = Incompetent

There is **no clear organizational plan** and/or **insufficient material**. The paper **might attempt** to **take a position**, but it **fails** to provide examples, fact, or rhetoric to support the position. Ideas are **not grouped logically**.

The paper may be **repetitious** with little or **no focus** on the general topic.

Sentence structure is **simple** and **generally erroneous** and **lacking variety**. Word choice is **simple**, **vague**, and **inexact**. The writer makes **no attempt** to choose the best words for the topic, audience, and purpose.

Surface errors are **frequent** and **extreme**, and **severely interfere** with the reader's understanding of the work.

Relevant State Standards

<u>Vocabulary Power Plus for the ACT: Book Three</u>

High School - Grade 9

These are only the minimum standards that the product line meets; if these standards seem out of order, they typically go in "keyword" order; from the Language Usage category of standards, to Comprehension, Analysis, Writing, Research/Applied, and Technology/Media categories. Therefore these standards may be in a different order than the order given by your local Department of Education. Also if one state standard meets multiple categories, that particular standard is listed the first time it appears, to reduce redundancy. Again, please refer to your local Department of Education for details on the particular standards.

Bias/Validity standards are included, as is Voice/Style standards, as both categories include use of words for different effects on the audience (connotation, denotation, distortion, formality, etc.) and thus are logical inclusions.

Depending on state, standards pertaining to use of dialect and idiomatic expressions might be met by this product. Please refer to your local Department of Education for details.

Notation is as close as possible to the notation given by the Department of Education of the respective state.

States:

Alabama:
Std. 34; Std. 1; Std. 5; Stds. 24-28; Std. 29; Std. 9; Stds. 20-22; Std. 13; Std. 14;
Std. 8; Std. 1; Std. 3; Std 4; Std. 6; Std. 23; Std. 9; Stds. 20-22

Alaska:
R4.1.1-4; R4.4.1-2; R4.5.1; R4.5.2-3; W4 (all); R4.1.5; R4.2.1-2; R4.3.1-4;
R4.3.5-6; R4.7.1; R4.9.2; R4.9.1; R4.6.1-4; R4.9.1; W4.2.2; W4.4.5

Arizona:
R1.4PO1; R1.4PO2-5; R1.6PO1-5; R3.2PO1-3; R3.1PO6; R2.1PO2, 4; W1
(all); W2.4-6 (all); W2.3.1-5; R3.3PO1-3; R1.6PO1-5; R3.1PO6; R2.2PO1;
R2.1PO3; W1.4PO4; W2.3.1-5

Arkansas:
R.11.10.1-4; R.10.10.1-2; R.10.10.19; R.9.10.13; W.4.10 (all); W.6.10 (all);
W.5.10 (all); W.7.10.8; R.9.10.3; R.9.10.6; R.9.10.8; R9.10.4; R.10.10.24;
W.4.10.13

California:
R1.1-2; R1.3; R2 (all); R3.7; R3.11; WOC1.1-5; W1.2; W2 (all); R3.12; R3.6-
10; R3 (entire)

Colorado (broad standards):
S1; S6; S2; S3; S4

Connecticut:
1.3 (all); 1.1 (all); 2.1 (all); 1.2g; 3.2 (all); 4.2 (all); 4.3 (all); 3.1 (all); 1.4
(all); 2.3 (entire); 2.1D

Delaware:
2.2a; 1.5; 2.4k; 2.4bL; 4.2b; 2.4bl/T; 4.2c; 1.1; 1.3; 1.2; 1.1, 1.5; 2.4j; 2.5f;
4.3A; 2.4G; 2.3A,C; 1.3; 1.2

District of Columbia:
10.LD-V.8-10; 10.LT-G.2; 10.LT-S.10; 10.LD-Q.4; 10.W-R.6; 10.EL.1-5;
10.LT-C.1; 10.LT-F.4-5; 10.LT.TN.12-13; 10.W-E.3-5

Florida (broad standards):
R.1 (all); R.2 (all); Li.1 (all); W.1 (all); W.2.3; La.1.2; LVS.1.4; Li.1.1; Li.1 and 2

Georgia:
ELA10RC3; ELA10RL5; ELA10RL1; ELA10W1; ELA10RL4; ELA10W2; ELA10RL3

Hawaii (broad standards):
S2; S1; S4; S5,6; S7; S3

Idaho:
10.LA.1.8.1-2; 10.LA.2.1 (all); 10.LA.4.2.3; 10.LA.2.2.2; 10.LA.1.2.2; 10.LA.2.3.5; 10.LA.3 (all); 10.LA.5.3, 4; 10.LA.4 (all); 10.LA.2.3.6; 10.LA.2.3.3; 9-12.Spch.6.3; 10.LA.2.3.4

Illinois:
1.A.4a; 1.A.4b; 1.B.4b; 1.C (all); 2.A.4d; 3.B.4b; 3.A.4; 3.B.4a; 1.B.4a; 1.B.4C; 2.B.4B; 2.A.4C; 3.B.4C

Indiana:
10.1.1-4; 10.2.3; 10.3.1; 10.2.1; 10.3.7-8; 10.4 (all); 10.6 (all); 10.5 (all); 10.3.11; 10.7.12; 10.3.12; 10.3.6; 10.3.2; 10.4.10-12

Iowa (Model Core Curriculum):
R6; R1; R3; W1; W7; W2, W3; R4; V3; R5; S7

Kansas:
RB3:1-3, 5; RB4:13; RB4:1; RB3:4; RB4:2-6, 9-10; RB4:14-15; LB1:2; RB4:11; LB2 (entire)

Kentucky (Academic Expectations):
AE1.2; AE2.30, 33; AE2.38; AE1.11; AE6.1, 2.25

Louisiana:
RR1.1; RR1.5; RR7.12; RR6.9; W2.19; WP3.25-29; W2.20-21; W2.18; W2.24; RR7.15; RR6.7; RR1.3; RR7.11

Maine:
A1; B7; B8, D4; A6; E1-3; F1-3; G4-5; G8; C7-8; H10-11; B5-6; B10-11; E1,4

Maryland (HAS documents used):
G3.2.2; G1.1.1-4; G1.1.5; G2.1 (all); G1.2.2-3; G3.1 (all); G3.3 (all); G2.1 (all); G1.3.3; G4.3.1; G2.3.3; G1.2.5; G1.2.4

Massachusetts:
4.23; 4.24; 4.25; 13.25; 15.7; 21.8; 5.23-28; 22.9; 25.5; 19.25; 20.5; 6.8-9;

24.5; 9.6; 8.29; 10.5; 3.16

Michigan (Michigan Merit Curriculum used):
3.3; 3.2; 1.1; 4.1; 1.3, 1.5; 2.1, 2.2; 2.3

Minnesota:
IB4-5; IB1-5; ID14; IC3; ID9; IC4; ID4-5; IIB1-8; IIC2-3; IIA1; IIC1; IIIB5-7, 9-10; IC8; ID15; ID1-3; ID12; IIIA7

Mississippi:
1a; 2a-d; 2e; 1b-d; 3a; 4a-c; 3b-d; 1B; 1C

Missouri:
I5c; II2b; II11; I6a-d; II3c; IV2d; I1c; II1a; I1a; II1b; II4a, c-h; II6a-b; II1a; II3a-b; I5B; I4A,C; II1D; II3A; II3A-B

Montana:
RCS2; RCS1; LCS1; RCS5; WCS2; WCS1; WCS4; RCS4; RCS3; LCS2; LCS5

Nebraska (standards set at grade 12):
12.1.1; 12.1.5; 12.1.6

Nevada (standards set at grade 12):
1.12.3; 1.12.4-5; 2.12.1-3; 4.12.6; 5.12.2; 3.12.7; 3.12.5-6; 6.12.1-5, 7; 7.12.1-5; 5.12.2-6; 3.12.3; 3.12.1; 8.12.2

New Hampshire:
R-10-1, 2, 3; R-10-13; R-10-7.1-3; R-10-4.4; R-10-7.5; R-10-4.5; R-10-6.1; W-10-10; W-10-1, 9; W-10-11.4; R-10-15.2; R-10-11.1-3

New Jersey:
3.1.F.1-3; 3.1.G.12-13; 3.2.D.6; 3.1.D.3; 3.2.B.1; 3.1.G.11; 3.1.G.6; 3.1.G.8; 3.2.A (all); 3.2.C (all); 3.2.B.5; 3.2.B.1; 3.2.D.2; 3.2.D.8; 3.1.E.1-3; 3.1.G.9; 3.1.H.6; 3.4.B.2-3; 3.5.B.1; 3.1.G.3; 3.1.G.5; 3.1.G.7; 3.2.A.6-7

New Mexico:
1C10-3; 3B10-3; 2A10 (all); 1C10-2; 3B10-1,2; 1A10-4; 2A10 (entire)

New York (broad standards):
ELA-S1, ELA-S2; ELA-S3

North Carolina:
6.01; 1.03; 2.01; 4.05; 6.01-02; 4.04

North Dakota:
10.2.1; 10.2.4; 10.6.2-3; 10.3.3-14; 10.6.1; 10.2.2; 10.6.5; 10.3.8

Ohio:
10-WC; 10-RP; 10-RA-IT; 10-RA-L; 10-WP; 10-WC; 10-WA

Oklahoma:
10-RL1 (all); 10-RL2-4c; 10-RL3-1a-b; 10-RL3-3a-c; 10-WM1 (all); 10-WM3 (all); 10-WM2 (all); 10-RL2-1c; 10-VL1-1; 10-RL2-1b, 4b; 10-RL3-4A; 10-RL3-2D-E; 10-RL3-4C; 10-WM1-6; 10-WM2-7C,8

Oregon:
EL.CM.RE.08-14; EL.CM.RE.15-18; EL.CM.RE.02; EL.CM.LI.13; EL.CM.WR.01-09; EL.CM.WR.10-20; EL.CM.WR.21-26; EL.CM.SL.01-09; EL.CM.RE.06; EL.CM.RE.27, 28, 31; EL.CM.LI.01; EL.CM.LI.11-14; EL.CM.LI.17-18; EL.CM.WR.07

Pennsylvania (standards set at grade 11):
1.1.11C; 1.1.11E-F; 1.1.11G; 1.1.11H; 1.1.11B; 1.3.11C; 1.5.11 (all); 1.4.11 (all); 1.1.11D; 1.3.11B; 1.4.11D-E

Rhode Island:
R-10-1, 2, 3; R-10-13; R-10-7.1-3; R-10-4.4; R-10-7.5; R-10-4.5; R-10-6.1; W-10-10; W-10-1, 9; W-10-11.4; R-10-15.2; R-10-11.1-3

South Carolina:
E2-R3.1-4; E2-R2.2; E2-R1.3; E2-W1.6.2-5; E2-R1.5; E2-R2.2, 4; E2-W1 (all); E2-W1.6.1; E2-W2 (all); E2-R1.7-9; E2-C3.7; E2-R1.4; E2-R2.1; E2-R5-6; E2-R2.3,6; E2-C1.13

South Dakota:
10.W.1.2; 10.R.2.2; 10.W.1.1; 10.W.3.1; 10.R.4.1-2; 10.R.3.1; 10.R.2.1

Tennessee (Learning Expectations):
2LE-3; 2LE-1; 4LE-10; 1LE-1; 2LE-4, 5, 8; 2LE-13; 2LE-14; 1LE- 5-10; 1LE-11; 1LE-2, 3, 4; 2LE-10; 2.2.E

Texas (TEKS section 110.43):
b6 (all); b7 (all); b8B; b11D; b12A; b2 (all); b3 (all); b12B-C; B8D; B9A; B11A,F; B5 (entire)

Utah:
1-O1 (all); 1-O2 (all); 1-O3e; 2-O3 (all); 3-O1c; 1-03a,e; 1-03 (entire)

Vermont:
R-10-1, 2, 3; R-10-13; R-10-7.1-3; R-10-4.4; R-10-7.5; R-10-4.5; R-10-6.1;
W-10-10; W-10-1, 9; W-10-11.4; R-10-15.2; R-10-11.1-3

Virginia:
10.4; 10.3; 10.7; 10.8; 10.3D; 10.9

Washington (EALRs used here):
R1.2; R2 (all); R3 (all); W2.4; W1 (all); W3.3; W2 (all); W3.2; W4.1

West Virginia (prefix for these citations: RLA):
O.10.1.10; O.10.1.04-06, 09; O.10.1.02; O.10.1.07; O.10.2.01-10; O.10.1.11;
O.10.1.01; O.10.1.08

Wisconsin (standards set at grade 12):
D.12.1; A.12.1; A.12.4; A.12.2; B.12.2; B.12.3; B.12.1; A.12.2-3

Wyoming:
R-IB; R-IA; R-IIIB2; R-IIA; R-IIIA; R-IIC; W-IB; W-IE, F, G; W-IA; W-IIA;
W-IIB; W-IIC; W-IID; W-ID; SL-1b; R-IIB2,5; SL-9